PASTOR, We Need A Bigger Boat

A Paradigm Shift for Reaching Today's Youth

by: Steve Fitzhugh

TOUCH PUBLISHING

Copyright © 2014 by Steve Fitzhugh

ISBN: 978-0-9919839-9-5

All rights reserved. No portion of this book may be reproduced, stored in a retrieval system, or transmitted in any form or by any means - electronic, mechanical, photocopy, recording, or any other, without prior written consent from the publisher.

Unless otherwise marked, Scripture quotations taken from the HOLY BIBLE, NEW INTERNATIONAL VERSION®. Copyright© 1973, 1978, 1984 by International Bible Society. Used by permission of Zondervan Publishing House. All rights reserved.

JAWS TM & © Universal Pictures (1975). References used pursuant to fair use doctrine of U.S. copyright laws.

Author photo by Robert Shanklin

Published by Touch Publishing
Requests should be directed to:
P.O. Box 180303
Arlington, Texas 76096
www.TouchPublishingServices.com

To schedule Steve Fitzhugh to bring a high-energy, engaging, passionate message to your next youth event, contact him through his website: www.PowerMoves.org

Library of Congress Control Number: 2014939224

Printed in the United States of America on acid-free paper

In dedication to Reverend Ronald J. Fowler

With eternal thanks, Brother Ron, for introducing me to Jesus Christ and training me to become a lifelong disciple. You modeled integrity in ministry, compassion for the lost, and you fanned the flame of passion for Christ within my young teenage heart. You accepted and encouraged my unique approach to ministry and gave me the confidence to always be myself. I, along with so many others, am bountifully grateful for your tremendous influence upon my life. I am humbly aware that the fruit I produce began long ago in the garden of a young heart, where you first planted good seed.

Steve Fitzhugh's commitment, dedication, and gifting to reach and impact the youth of today has been demonstrated over a number of years and makes him more than qualified to speak to how churches can reach today's youth. You will find his book *Pastor, We Need A Bigger Boat* engaging, enlightening, and empowering. If you want to make a difference in reaching youth, read this book!

Pastor John K. Jenkins, Sr.
First Baptist Church of Glenarden, Maryland

I have had the privilege of witnessing Steve Fitzhugh's incredible ministry to youth for over 25 years. It is amazing to see how the Lord uses him to reach all kinds of students, no matter where or who they are. He is always relevant and extremely gifted and has proven insight on how to effectively serve America's youth.

Charles Whitaker, Senior Pastor
River of Life Church, Marlow Heights, Maryland

Steve Fitzhugh is one of the finest, most gifted communicators in the country. It is an opinion I developed while witnessing him in action and seeing audience responses. He is hilarious, artful, and authentic – integrating his entire body to launch his thoughts and ideas. A national treasure. Even though I hate the "R" word, *Bigger Boat* is RELEVANT for local church leadership. Steve presents clear solutions that connect with youth. This is out-of-the-box thinking for every pastor serious about the church of tomorrow!

Joel A. Freeman, Ph.D.
CEO/President, The Freeman Institute

If there is any one reality that all pastors are aware of it is that times and things are changing. How do we reach, enlist, and engage the next generation? Many have sought to answer that question, but most have fallen short. Into that wide area of need comes this book.
Steve Fitzhugh is not a theorist, he is a practitioner. When he writes, he does so with a pen sharpened on the anvil of experience. Fitzhugh knows his stuff. This book paints a picture and points the way for us, as pastors, to minister to this present age.

Timothy J. Clarke
Senior Pastor, First Church of God, Columbus, OH

Contents

Introduction	1
Chapter 1 - The Closest to the Water	15
Chapter 2 - Terror in Amity	25
Chapter 3 - Why the Youth?	35
Chapter 4 - The Journey Begins	47
Chapter 5 - Shady Strategy	59
Chapter 6 - The Super Hero	73
Chapter 7 - Hooper Brings the Edge	87
Chapter 8 - As Goes the Head, So Goes the Body	99
Chapter 9 - Who's on Watch?	115
Chapter 10 - The End-ing	121
About the Author	135
Also by Steve Fitzhugh	136

Introduction

The greatest challenge facing Christian churches today is the task of successfully engaging, educating, and evangelizing the next generation. In church-speak this group is called "the youth." I believe with all my heart that the benchmark of relevance for any church is its ability to attract, disciple, and send forth youth infused with purpose to be kingdom citizens; men and women equipped and ready to be ambassadors for Jesus.

It's fair to say that if your church is anemic in this area, then you have a problem. You might not be fully cognizant of the magnitude of this problem at the moment, but ten, fifteen, or twenty years from now it will be glaringly obvious. The hopes and dreams of our future are predicated on our success in this one vital area. The safety and security of our children and grandchildren and the sustained viability of our schools and communities also depend on those who have godly influence on the mindset and heart of today's youth.

Ironically, most leaders would agree with such a premise. However, agreement and action are two separate realities. Pastors are quick to articulate a commitment to reach the youth and they subsequently welcome the applause of such convictions. The youth hear these promises declared, but too often are disappointed when they don't come to pass. The last thing today's youth need is the disappointment of empty promises. The question we must ask is whether or not the "talk" will ever match the "walk" in these declarations. Until Bible leather turns into shoe leather, words and wishes are unwelcome by our young people. One might think that with such broad consensus of necessary and needed focus on the youth that churches and their leaders would demonstrate their commitment with follow-through.

One tangible vehicle in which this commitment could be reflected is in the youth ministry line item of a church's annual budget. Another is the extent to which the designated finances invested in youth-specific paid staff are protected. Are these finances viewed as an *expectation* rather than an *expendable extra*? With youth at the fulcrum of the success and failure of our faith communities, and considering the priority of youth in God's global economy, it could be supposed that church leadership would be quick to explore beyond the limits of the norm and think creatively what it will take to accomplish its goals pertaining to the outreach, programming, and discipleship of our youth.

Tragically this is not the case. Typically, too many churches treat the youth program as a modest option for investment. And when compared to the church's overall budgeting dollars, the youth line item is nominal at best, if it is even a consideration at all.

Ray Lewis, one time perennial All-Pro linebacker for the Baltimore Ravens of the National Football League, found himself in crisis before his career ever really took off. It was while facing two first-degree murder charges, sitting alone in a jail cell, indicted, that for the first time ever he heard a whisper in his ear that changed his life forever: "Can you hear me now?"

He's been listening to that voice and doing what it asks of him ever since. The Church is in crisis! To each of us God is saying, "Can you hear me now?"

Are we listening?

Students are on a rampage, bullying defenseless classmates. Teen violence is perpetrated against defenseless victims, like the elderly and the homeless. Drug abusers, alcohol users, rape and murder victims are masked in youthful faces. Instead of preparing for bright futures, they find themselves casualties of their own bad decisions. Parents are at the end of their rope, uncertain of how to engage their distant teenager and, in some cases, even afraid to confront inappropriate behavior. It is no wonder teachers in the schools can't get students to be respectful and obedient, teens disrespect and disobey their own parents at home!

Crisis!

Television, the music industry, and music videos all saturate our youth with compromising thoughts and actions. Hostile and aggressive video games dominate the time and attention of our youngest children. Their young minds are desensitized to the unfathomable. They accept that which they should abhor.

Crisis!

Social media allows students to exist in an unmonitored virtual reality where they experiment with taboo thoughts and topics. Through the World Wide Web students are just a few mouse clicks away from unfettered access to a world of pornographic addiction. Graduation rates are declining.

Crisis!

Teen abortion is on the rise. Teen parenting is a norm. Every two hours and sixteen minutes a teenager commits suicide in America. For every successful suicide, there are dozens of failed attempts. Families fractured by that one reprobate, rogue sibling find it difficult to even answer the phone not knowing whether or not the voice on the other end is going to report tragedy or devastation.

Crisis!

Teens are unequipped to handle the stress in their lives and cut themselves, searching for relief. They self-medicate with harmful temporary solutions including, but not limited to, prescription pills, drunkenness, and promiscuity.

Crisis!

We have been forewarned that the last days would bring unprecedented evil. In the New Testament, Paul exhorts his spiritual son Timothy by saying,

> *But mark this: There will be terrible times in the last days. People will be lovers of themselves, lovers of money, boastful, proud, abusive, disobedient to their parents, ungrateful, unholy, without love, unforgiving, slanderous, without self-control, brutal, not lovers of the good, treacherous, rash, conceited, lovers of pleasure rather than lovers of God—having a form of godliness but denying its power. Have nothing to do with such people.*
>
> *(2 Timothy 3:1-5)*

Paul warned us that it would be bad, but who could imagine the callousness, hardness, commitment to self-gratifying lusts, and bold rebellion which we witness among America's youth today? Unattended, it's destined to worsen. Our students have become victims of church leadership who are ill-equipped to lead. Our students are sheep who need a shepherd that speaks their language and identifies with their culture, their needs, and their world. If we who are responsible for them do not take heed and make provisions, their fate is sealed—sadly they will become the victims of adult dysfunction.

Many parents are oblivious to the secret risky exploits practiced by a son or daughter living under the same roof and sitting night by night at the same dinner table. They think all is well. But all is not well. We are in crisis!

Too many leaders have their heads in the sand and proceed with their personal agendas, thinking a band-aid is a sufficient remedy for this generation already living in catastrophe. In light of this war against our children, how has the church responded? The institution which throughout time has been the great equalizer, the Church, suffers from a frightful disconnect with today's youth in today's culture. The worldly competition for the time and attention of our students is so intense that most church-based approaches to reach and teach our youth are simply irrelevant, antiquated, and, in many cases, laughable. And when outdated efforts are offered in a feeble attempt to connect, they fail miserably. A student stained by an inappropriate encounter with an impotent, lame youth ministry will probably never return.

Most church events commonly include music as a quintessential element of the program. This is especially true with youth. I recently attended a youth function where the best music the church could offer was played in the fellowship hall on a boom box with a microphone positioned in front of it. Believe it or not, the music player only played cassette tapes! CASSETTE TAPES! Next to the boom box was a case of dated cassettes. Now in fairness, it may have been the case that the boom box was the best that they could do.

However, a quick inventory of other church expenditures proved such a presupposition false. Few pastors are willing to push the envelope to finance a youth pastor and commit to an unwavering youth ministry budget.

My response begins with Scripture: "We are hard pressed on every side, but not crushed; perplexed, but not in despair." (2 Corinthians 4:8)

There is an answer, there is a solution to even the greatest challenge. Our divine architect has available through His word every resource needed to break the mold, change the game, rescue our youth, and help build up kingdom-minded, spiritually grounded young ambassadors for change. I know this because it is in God's word. God said it and I believe it. And is there anything more powerful than the word of God? No. I tell you again, there is nothing more powerful than the word of God! I have always believed that, but is it scripturally the case?

Jesus replied, "And why do you break the command of God for the sake of your tradition? For God said, 'Honor your father and mother and anyone who curses their father or mother is to be put to death.' But you say that if anyone declares that what might have been used to help their father or mother is 'devoted to God,' they are not to 'honor their father or mother' with it. Thus you **nullify** *(emphasis mine) the word of God for the sake of your tradition. You hypocrites! Isaiah was right when he prophesied* about you:

> *"These people honor me with their lips,*
> *but their hearts are far from me.*
> *They worship me in vain;*
> *their teachings are merely human rules."*
> *(Matthew 15:3-9)*

What does nullify mean? According to Merriam-Webster, nullify is defined as "to make something legally null; to cause something to lose its value or have no effect."

What stronghold is retarding the advance and nullifying the word of God in the lives of youth and ministry to youth? Tradition! Some churches are so anchored to protocol and tradition they are unwilling to budge. I have witnessed it firsthand.

Standing in the pulpit one Friday night for a "Youth Explosion" I noticed most of the teens sitting in the very back of the sanctuary. The deacons, clad in their black suits, filled the first two rows. Before I began my youth presentation I asked if the deacons would allow the teens to populate the first two rows. After all, it was their event. The teens had raised the money to cover all of the expenses of the event to expose their peers to a youth-specific ministry style bringing a relevant word from God.

The deacons absolutely refused to move. They laughed at me and looked at me as if I had lost my mind. The students even stood, eagerly anticipating coming to the front. I could tell they felt special because they were singled out to come to a prominent place in the church. The deacons would not budge. In my mind's eye, it was as if tradition had chained these deacons to the front pew and ego had thrown away the key.

After some awkward pleading and encouragement from the new pastor, the deacons relented, to which the rest of the congregation applauded. It was not a cheerful relenting; they begrudgingly gave up their coveted, traditional seating arrangement. The youth left the back of the church on their special night, and filled up the front of their church. The looks on their faces were priceless.

It is standard practice to offer evaluations or some thought-out vehicle for feedback at the conclusion of special events, programs, or conferences. Annual evaluations are even done for routine tasks to allow opportunity for improvement moving forward. After all, only that which is measured can be improved. Evaluation is a proven way to determine what works and what doesn't, or what is effective and what is not. Let me ask, when was the last time you invited your congregation to evaluate or comment on your youth program? Unfortunately, within our churches, formal evaluation seems to be the most underutilized tool for growth and health. When done properly and taken seriously, evaluation can lead to strengthening performance and production. Outreaches, strategies, and programs seem to be birthed all the time, but rarely receive the kind of annual critical evaluation needed to confirm continuation, make adjustments or identify the need for elimination.

Joe Gibbs, former head coach of the Washington Redskins, experienced Super Bowl success. He was noted for not only building championship teams, but championship men. One key element of his success was his willingness to make halftime adjustments to his game-day strategy. How have you adjusted your strategy to save your youth? That isn't to say that God has not imparted anointed initiatives for a certain time, for a certain place, and for a certain people! But is God so limited that he must use the same paradigm to reach the lost for every time, every place and every people? I would say not!

Times change, people change, norms change, and culture changes. The truths of God never change, but how we present the truth may need to change so the truth can be heard.

Why then do churches embrace the same exhausted approaches to outreach—and specifically youth ministry—that were used thirty years ago? Ten years ago? Five years ago? Because of tradition! Tradition is comfortable, safe, and proven. Initially the paradigm was successful. It produced fruit. It was done again and again for years with the same results. But when was the last time you audited those efforts? Is it producing the same fruit today? When have you last examined your approach, or evaluated what you've come to accept simply as, "the way we do things here at this church"? Certainly there has been cultural change in the last thirty years that would demand we reexamine our approach to ministry through the filter of contemporary culture? Could it be that the reason youth work at your church is on life-support is because it is time for a change?

"Ah," but you say, "it's about Christ, not the culture."

Jesus would beg to differ with you. As you already know, He leveraged culture in most of His efforts to communicate the truths of the kingdom. For instance, He lived in an agriculturally-based society, so He talked about farmers sowing seeds, vines, pruning, reaping, and harvesting.

When Jesus saw Peter and the other fishermen consumed within their trade, Jesus had to think to himself, "Hmm, I can use that." He then called them to be "fishers of men." He spoke of casting nets, launching into the deep, and fishing. These "plain sight" elements were consistent with the culture and his time.

To the woman at the well He talked about water; to the fishermen He talked about fishing for men. One of the most popular trades (of which he was also a part) was carpentry. The carpenters made wooden yokes. Custom yokes assured that oxen could work comfortably. So Jesus discussed how His yoke is easy and His burden light. Instead of leaning toward his own devices, it appears Jesus looked at the world around him and imagined how he could use the plain, the ordinary, and the commonplace of His time to expound upon his message.

Should we not take His cue and assess our world to find relevant paradigms that capture the attention of today's youth and then use our imagination to employ them? Sadly, we do not. It has become easier and safer to trust tradition. Although the youth are touted as the church of tomorrow, today, when it counts most, they are a budgetary after-thought. Less than 1% of the average church's annual budget is allotted for the youth program (outside of salary). Only one of every twenty churches even has a paid youth staffer. In most churches, ministry to the youth is an unpaid proposition assigned to a quasi-interested volunteer, who happened to be standing in the wrong place at the wrong time. Youth ministry suffers today and the outlook for tomorrow is bleak.

The challenge at this juncture is not necessarily to kindle the fire of passion for ministry to youth within the youth minister and the pastor. The fervor and intent to serve and minister to this audience certainly already exists. They both want to see the gospel spread and lives changed among the youth. It's all about perspectives. The pastor is typically consumed with the ministry of shepherding the flock and the business of ministry needed to sustain the church as an organization. The time and energy of the youth worker includes, but is not limited to, preaching, teaching, building relationships with the youth, hearing their problems, serving as their counselor, and visiting their world on school campuses. Consequently, the person with the greatest sensitivity as to what it's going to take to reach the youth will be he or she who is closest to them.

I like to parallel the classic movie *JAWS* in my assessment of the condition of our churches and their commitment to the youth of this millennium because there is a "shark" terrorizing your students. In *JAWS* it was the person who was closest to the water who first saw the shark. I believe that youth ministers, who are the closest to the predators of our youth, are also the ones who can best assess what is needed to kill the shark. They are crying out for help. In *JAWS*, the man who first recognizes the enormity of the problem cries out, "We are going to need a bigger boat!"

Can you hear your own youth minister calling out? I bet you can. If the one who is in and around the water frequently says, "We need a bigger boat!" let's trust that voice. Let's get him a bigger boat. Let's help him develop a new paradigm.

For over thirty years, I've been close—in, under, and around the water of the youth of America. I've seen the dimensions of the shark that's terrorizing your students. I've devoted most of my adult life documenting snares set for our youth and rescuing our disadvantaged teens from complacency and delinquency; bringing them to new life, hope, and productivity. I've buried far too many good kids and have been forced to visit far too many students locked away in our penal systems. I have heard more heart-gripping stories than I care to recount of teenage tragedy.

At my peak as an assembly speaker, I averaged over 150 middle and senior high campus visits a year as the national spokesman for the Fellowship of Christian Athletes One Way 2 Play Drug-Free Assembly Program. I've engaged over a million students in America. Hear me when I say that when it comes to the typical local church paradigm to reach youth: "Pastor, we need a bigger boat!"

We need local pastoral leadership with the courage to make a paradigm shift in their approach and execution of ministry to youth and community. Many existing youth ministry prototypes are irrelevant and devoid of impact and anointing. My hope is that at the end of this book you, too, will not only agree that we need a bigger boat—you'll commit to doing what it takes to get one.

Chapter 1 | The Closest to the Water

In the summer of 1975, the movie *JAWS* hit the big screen. Not only was it a summer movie phenomenon, it terrorized beach-goers and has continued to do so for years. I am sure that the theme music alone still provokes nightmares in many people. It became the highest-grossing movie of its time and won three Oscars and nine other awards. With all of this success, you'd think perhaps it had a complicated, intricate plot. The truth is quite the opposite. The plot is very simple.

A gigantic great white shark begins to menace the small island community of Amity. A police chief, a marine scientist, and a grizzled fisherman set out to stop it. I must admit, after seeing *JAWS* I was afraid to go to the beach or even dip my feet into a lake. And

Pastor, We Need A Bigger Boat!

forget about braving the open water! As these three set out to kill the great white, they were assigned duties to be fulfilled during the quest. Quint, the boat's owner and captain, kept an eye out for the predator. Hooper, the marine scientist, drove the boat. Chief Brody maintained the chum line. By far, the most unpleasant task was shoveling chum (bloody fish bait) over the back of the boat. But it had to be done. The hopes were that the shark would pick up on the blood scent and reveal itself. Understandably, Chief Brody hated this task.

Now picture this: Chief Brody is sitting on the back of the boat shoveling bloodied chum out of a bucket into the ocean. He is mumbling to himself, complaining about the work, when suddenly, the biggest great white shark he had ever seen, the movie's star adversary, bursts from the surface of the water. It lunges at the chief with mouth open wide and narrowly misses receiving a mouthful of the chief's head. With his face void of color, the chief stands. Numb, unable to speak, he stumbles into the hull of the boat in a daze. He blindly grasps for the radio and calls, "Mayday! Mayday! Help, this is *The Orca*!"

Quint grabs the radio from the chief in defiant arrogance.

"What are you doing Chief?" Quint questions.

"I think we are going to need a bigger boat," the chief replies with insistence in his voice. "WE'RE GOING TO NEED A BIGGER BOAT!"

"We don't need no bigger boat!" Quint responds,

brushing off the demand. "I've been catching sharks for twenty years on this boat. We don't need no bigger boat."

This sequence of events provides the background for what became one of the movie's most memorable lines and my inspiration for the title of this book. When Chief Brody's request for a bigger boat was vetoed by Quint, frustration set in Chief Brody's face and disbelief in his heart. For the purposes of our analogy, the chief represents a type of a seasoned youth pastor. I can imagine his frustration. I have felt his disappointment. It comes when you want to make an impact with a different, relevant ministry style that is adapted to be effective to the current culture of the youth, only to have your effort extinguished by someone in authority. The frustration rears again when you recognize that the extent of your need is greater than the commitment of resources allocated to respond to it. It burns hot when you are consumed with a godly passion to serve youth, but are consistently limited by the absence of resources, support or allies.

Quint represents a type of a pastor as well, one we will refer to as the all-encompassing "powers that be." In some churches, the pastor doesn't have the final say. But nearly all churches have someone with the kind of authority (spoken or unspoken) to open doors no man can shut and close doors no man (in some cases seemingly even God) can open. Quint represents that kind of authority on the boat. After all, it is his boat, and he did broker the deal with the Amity city officials to catch the shark. That's exactly where many pastors forfeit true vision for their church. Execution of their vision is limited by the approval or disapproval of unofficial leaders. We are in need of church leadership more committed to identifying with the interests of God, rather than satisfying reasonable and practical agendas of man.

Getting this part right begins with leadership acknowledging the rightful owner of the church. It is not your church. It's God's church, and you are the under-shepherd. Instead, we find churches ill-equipped to reach this generation, who miss the mark, and remain lost because of spiritual disobedience. Their authority prevents them from distinguishing between doing *good* things or doing *God's* things.

The pastor's first obligation should be to steward Jesus' bride, the Church, in an attempt to present her to the bridegroom prepared for eternity without spot, wrinkle, or blemish. This cannot be done without God's help. The first obligation is not to cling to one's authority. This is what Quint failed to realize when he overruled the chief. Chief Brody was the closest to the water when the shark first emerged. Chief Brody had a front row seat. It all happened in a flash, but he was able to peer into the shark's mouth. He marveled at the size of the humongous teeth, the girth of its torso, and the reach of its gaping man-eating jaws that were undoubtedly responsible for the ghastly severing of the head and shoulders of Amity's first victim, washed ashore by an unforgiving tide. Being closest to the water placed Chief Brody in the greatest vantage point to offer a first-hand, informed, up-close description of the challenge of the catch. It doesn't matter how long men had been catching sharks around Amity, *this* shark was different. The chief understood that and recognized that their approach, expectations, and vessel were all inadequate. This was a great white shark of unprecedented length and weight. It was clearly twenty to twenty-five feet long and weighed about two tons. His conclusion was overwhelmingly clear: "We need a bigger boat!" After witnessing just one pass of the shark, the chief was convinced that the vessel was in the right place, but was insufficient to see the assignment through. It didn't matter that *The Orca* housed the hopes that it would aid in killing the shark. It simply wasn't the right vessel for the magnitude of that particular job.

Many churches are in the right place and headed in the right direction, but their strategy is flawed and insufficient. Defiant, self-serving leadership cling tightly to personal agendas and render themselves ignorant to the scope of the hunt. As such, they extinguish the relevant ideas that may actually afford a reasonable opportunity for success.

I will never forget a great idea I had in the early years of my work at our youth center, called The House, in southeast Washington, D.C.

For several years in a row, a local school had experienced a rash of violence during its evening homecoming dances. They made a change. Instead of an evening dance, they decided to hold the homecoming dance right after school, in the school's gymnasium. The hope was that by having the dance during the daytime, it would diminish the risk of violent interruption by unauthorized attendees.

"Wouldn't it be a great idea," I thought, "to take my camera and go over to the school and take some homecoming dance photos of our students?"

Feeling happy-go-lucky, I grabbed my camera and walked over to the school. I paid my donation at the door and proceeded to the dance floor in the gym. There, I was absolutely undone. My mouth fell open and I couldn't believe my eyes. It was my "Chief Brody" moment. The vision I had anticipated of sweet, happy kids dancing face-to-face (as I remembered it from my day) was replaced with couples dancing so provocatively that the only thing that prevented actual sexual intercourse from happening was the fact that they had clothes on.

There was bumping and grinding of every sort. Some were standing, some were on the floor, as if they were alone in a bedroom. Boys were kissing boys, girls kissing girls, girls kissing boys, and boys kissing girls. I saw one young student lying on her back in the center of the floor while her dance partner, another female, laid on top of her as they "freaked" to the beat of the music. It took about five minutes for my brain to absorb everything I saw. I tucked my camera away, reluctant to take any photos so as not to be labeled a voyeur. Standing there, I saw into the mouth of the shark. I saw its size and the strength of its teeth.

My shock and awe were not limited to what I saw on the dance floor. I was equally stunned at the unresponsive disposition of the school staff, security, and chaperones. Surely they saw what I saw. Why weren't they saying something, doing something, or interrupting these students in their folly? Could it be that they had accepted the dismal fate of these misguided teens? Or had they simply conceded defeat, exhausted from years of unsuccessfully trying to make a difference? Or even worse, had they deemed that the students were "too far gone," as one principal stated?

At any rate, my first thought was, "We need a bigger boat!" In that moment I became like Chief Brody trapped on *The Orca*, radioing for help.

It doesn't have to be a shiny boat, a red boat, or a blue boat with a bell on top. It doesn't have to be a certain make, style, or price range. We simply need a bigger boat. The plan we devised to reach this generation was well-vetted, thought-out, and proven, but obviously far inferior to the task at hand. We were in the right place and headed in the right direction, but our strategy was insufficient. Our paradigm lacked precision and relevancy. At this homecoming dance in southeast Washington, D.C., at one of the city's most underserved high schools, I was not only close to the water, I was *in* the water. I sensed my own vulnerability amongst a ruthless predator seeking to kill, steal, and destroy. My heart began a thunderous ache. It almost took my breath away. Most of the girls there had their backs to their dance partners, while it appeared to me that their partners were trying to start a fire by friction by rubbing their pelvises against the backside of their mates with as much intensity as possible.

The DJ spewed x-rated suggestions from his turntables at deafening decibels. Adult innuendos riding upon relentless seductive rhythms lyrically stormed the ear gates of these minors. My students were in another world, in what seemed to be an impenetrable trance-like state.

This is but one glaring example of how we will fail to reach this generation forever if we do not employ a more advanced paradigm. This is what youth pastors and those who work with youth are faced with today. I am telling you Pastor, we need a bigger boat!

Can you hear the desperate pleas from the youth workers under your tutelage who are searching for solutions? *"How can I reach them? What can I use? Give me direction, Pastor. We need a bigger boat! How do I compete with the glitter and glare of this music and video-driven generation when the sound system at our church is not even as good as the one bumping in the trunk of some of our students' cars?"*

Do you hear it? More importantly, can you hear the cry of the Holy Spirit over a generation lost? We need a bigger boat!

Questions for reflection:

1. When is the last time you and your church's advisors evaluated the effectiveness of your youth program?

2. What pleas for help have your youth minister, or youth volunteers brought to you?

3. When presented with pleas for help, how do you respond? Do you take them seriously or see the requests as "one more budget item" that you aren't sure how to address?

4. Have you seen into the mouth of the shark that is terrorizing your church's youth?

5. If you haven't seen into the shark's mouth, what steps can you take to get up close and begin to analyze what you are dealing with?

Chapter 2
Terror in Amity

The discovery of a dismembered female body was part of the opening scene in the movie *JAWS*, bringing terror and intrigue to the first emergency responders.

What could do such incredible damage to a human body? How did it happen? Will it happen again? It was a great white shark! But great whites don't frequent the beaches of Amity. It couldn't be a great white!

Chief Brody, the investigator of this mystery, concludes that the remains were the result of a shark attack and he begins making preparations to close the beaches. Upon hearing the results of the report, the mayor becomes quite concerned. He's not as upset over the impending shark danger (as you would expect), but rather over the negative impact such a report would have on the summer beach economy.

The mayor insisted that the death was not the work of a shark, but rather the result of a boating tragedy. The mayor was well aware of the real cause, yet his publicly declared conclusion couldn't have been further from the truth. In the political world, calling this a boating accident is what politician handlers would call his positive "spin" on a negative situation.

When darkness is on the horizon and threatens the status quo, those who want to maintain the status quo, or avoid embarrassment or conflict, are quick to enter into denial. The mayor saw the bite marks, yet gave in to faulty judgment and ridiculously insisted it was a boating accident. The medical examiner initially concluded that it was a shark attack but amended his findings after the mayor cornered him for a private conversation. This was a classic case of manipulation and denial. Was it not the apostle Paul who said that the weapons of our warfare are not carnal but mighty for the demolishing of strongholds and pulling down of every high thing? Another translation puts it as pulling down every pretension that exalts itself above God. Our reasoning becomes that "high thing" or "skyscraper" that blocks out the intentions of God. When a pastor allows the truth to be blocked out, every step taken will be taken in darkness.

"No, this isn't happening at my church," one might say.

"Our youth don't use drugs."

"Youth in our church aren't being promiscuous!"

I personally know of students who lost their virginity at church while mom was in choir rehearsal!

Denial.

But denial isn't the only technique pastors use to avoid dealing with the challenges facing their youth. Those inside the church walls sometimes seek to hide the problem. For example, we keep it a secret when the quiet family at church discloses in confidence that their daughter is suicidal. Or when a panicked mom reveals that her son must meet with a judge because he took a gun to school, we treat her cries as an aberration and we don't even address it with the youth pastor. Pastors often try to solve the issue behind closed doors, oblivious to the comprehensive nature of the problem. The devil doesn't really have to spend much of his time destroying churches. Pastors, blind to the carnage washing up on their shores, foster their church's self-destruction because of their lack of response to unchecked teenage compromise. The devil does not come at us with a cape and a pitchfork. Secrecy is the might of his power.

Our first mistake comes when we attempt to hide, cover, or deny. Either we have forgotten or we fail to realize that the demonic strongholds in our congregations thrive in darkness. Hidden woe and unchecked issues choke out the life of the church unaware. The use of spiritual warfare language doesn't even make it to the pulpit for many congregations. Why? Because spiritual warfare doesn't pack our pews as well as the sermon topics that make us feel good, shout, and give our seed offering Sunday after Sunday. Whether we choose to preach about it our not, demonic activity is at the core. In fact, it showed up the moment we chose Jesus. Demons don't like the agitation or irritation they feel when faced with the power of Christ's light. Their anger burns when there is confrontation with truth, or exposure to extended, authentic praise and worship. Thus, the devil is relentless. He will not stop. His mission is to kill, steal, and destroy, over and over again. He must make the most of his opportunities because his time is short. So he acts immediately. I recall Jesus set that same example for the church when he discovered moneychangers in the temple? He recognized the disorder, intrusion, and darkness. He didn't cross his fingers and hope things would change. No! He took immediate action! Once the darkness was exposed, he drove the darkness out.

That great white shark was on a feeding frenzy in Amity and wasn't going to just wander off to some uninhabited beach. He was going to stay in Amity to feast until the feast was over. Those in authority did not have the luxury of non-action, but non-action was the luxury they took. It cost them dearly with the continued loss of life. The shark's early advantage was the denial by the decision makers that he even existed. When it comes to our congregations, it's not that we need to necessarily make all of the private battles that our families are fighting a matter of public knowledge. We do, however, need to have targeted, effective ministry designed to address the assault on our youth in order to eradicate the enemy at the breaches. Has that unexpected teen turned up pregnant at your church yet? Were you surprised to discover a member's young son was also now a father? Did you learn too late that there is a teen who is privately grieving from an abortion? They all need ministering. What foundation of relationship do they have with your youth ministry that affords them intimate access to God to process their pain, their shame, and their issues?

For every four of your students who are sexually active, one of them is carrying a sexually transmitted infection. How are your youth being served in this capacity? You'd be foolish to think your church's teens are immune from the devil's sabotage. From the time the school bell rings at the end of the school day until dinnertime, eleven million unsupervised students will be home alone, privy to everything television, radio, and the internet have to offer. Pastor, are you aware of that? How are you responding? If a student has a year of perfect attendance for church and if the average sermon is thirty minutes in length, that makes only twenty-six hours a year of godly teaching. What instruction fills the other 8,734 hours of the year?

Where there is a regular, even modest, youth group attendance the percentage of students using drugs, smoking weed, and engaging in risky behavior drops significantly. You need to be transparent about the intensity of the battle. If you aren't, all of Zion will know. Your student numbers will be too embarrassingly low to report and catastrophe among your youth will be unmistakably visible. When calling attention to the plight of the inadequate parenting in poor inner cities, Bill Cosby was told not to "air (their) dirty laundry in public" by these same parents. Bill Cosby responded by saying, "Your dirty laundry gets out of school at 2:30 p.m. everyday and is disruptive on the bus, disrespectful to adults, and is walking home cussing and starting fights."

If you choose to bury your head in the sand and wish your problems away, they will grow with a vengeance. There are serious issues confronting your youth. It can be tempting to proceed as if these issues will resolve themselves. They won't. And it takes more than a periodic special program. There must be a comprehensive strategy. Times have changed. Efforts to reach our youth must not be about numbers, attendance, or tithes. This is a matter of life and death. Too many good students, who grew up in the church, are buried young or make decisions that sabotage their future. Too many graduates head off to college never to be seen again on the radar of anyone's worship experience. Too many grandmothers in our pews find themselves the primary caregiver for a teenager they have absolutely no idea of how to reach. Laser tag and moon-bounce may entertain, but the task to disciple can only be accomplished within the bigger picture of a structured youth program. It's irresponsible for our churches to proceed without a bona fide, cogent plan to educate, disciple, and redeem our youth.

In Amity, the terror did not stop ... it spread. Shark attacks continued in this small beach town. The terror bred fear. Shop owners became afraid that closing the beaches until the shark was caught would cause them to lose money. The mayor was afraid that his aspirations for a new term in office would be jeopardized by the lack of tourists. Fear paralyzes. Fear keeps you from acting.

For the pastor it's the fear of the unknown. "How do I establish this comprehensive program? How many of our core members will disapprove of disbanding our traditional youth ministry efforts in lieu of a fresh approach?" This fear provokes a youth minister to keep a tight, two-fisted grip on his approach to do youth ministry, choking out reformation. One must not be timid about releasing that grip and allowing the organic process of new and exciting ministry to breathe.

I saw organic ministry in action years ago with one youth pastor's approach and I took note. He invited me to speak at his gathering. I checked the date and confirmed my availability. He then said he would meet me at his church at 5:30 a.m. I thought he was joking, but he was completely serious. His youth gathering was on Thursday mornings and was called the Thursday Morning Breakfast Club (TMBC). On the day that I was there, Jim Byrne had gathered six hundred high school students from area schools for the breakfast outreach. It was remarkable! It was the product of the mind of a youth pastor who had been given the latitude to dream, grow and evangelize the youth. Picture this, 600 TEENAGERS met to hear the gospel at 6:00 a.m.!

The shark's first victim had attended a beach party when she and a love interest headed to the waters for a late night swim. She made it to the waters but her boyfriend was too intoxicated to even remove his clothes and make it past the shores. As the shark attacked the girl, the boy, drunk, couldn't even hear her shrieks of terror and screams for help. Our youth are under attack from a great white shark and are screaming, "Help!" and we can't even hear them.

We have pastors who are drunk on the beach, intoxicated by their own ego and agenda, deaf to the voices of the desperate youth minister crying for funding. I've even encountered senior pastors who were obviously jealous of the young and exciting youth minister. Instead of mentoring the young theologian, the pastor, who is intimidated and insecure, withholds knowledge and insights that otherwise would expedite growth and development. Afraid to lose the congregation's favor to a younger voice, the pastor instead allows the young minister to struggle and suffer ineffectiveness.

Dr. Myles Munroe says, "One of the greatest failures of leadership is the failure to groom a successor."

Unfortunately it takes a tragedy that strikes close to home to open our eyes and ears to our resident deficiencies. The mayor continued to manipulate his "yes men" and construct roadblocks the chief could not hurdle. He even successfully convinced the medical examiner to alter his report. The official report erroneously concluded that the first victim suffered injuries consistent with a boating accident. The mayor of Amity continued his denial until it was his son found on the same beach. Why do we have to wait for a personal catastrophe before we are willing to find a way to deal with the shark and find the resources to see a committed solution prevail? There is good news: We don't have to wait.

Questions for reflection:

1. When faced with a crisis in your congregation, are you faced with the temptation to cover up or deny the problem?

2. Think back to the last youth crisis that happened within your church's youth. How was it handled?

3. What intervention techniques are in place to address the threats on your youth?

4. Who are the key members of your church leadership that need to be a part of the crisis management team, so when tragedy strikes, your plan is in place?

Chapter 3 | Why the Youth?

The second gruesome attack in Amity was on a young boy named Alex Kitner. He was out on a raft, in the water like everyone else, splashing and kicking. He was doing what young boys do and that in itself set him up to be a victim. Youth are the enemy's prime targets. Why? Because they are ultra-critical to the life and advancement of the church and the kingdom of God. Every revival has always begun with the youth. Young people are full of energy, ideas, and zeal. An influx of youth in any environment is going to change the dynamics simply because of the nature of their presence.

Students are the first to ask, "Why do we have to do it this way every time?" Adults are more apt to conform into obedient "sheeple" and go with the flow. Youth, on the other hand, are opinionated and willing to offer their point of view with or without an invitation. As such, they don't have to do anything special to make Satan's hit list. They already appear in his crosshairs, because they are young and full of godly potential.

When the disciples shooed the children away from Jesus, He sternly rebuked them. Children hold a special place in the heart of the master. Jesus scolded his disciples, "Suffer the children not!" Jesus went on to explain that unless we become like children we can't enter the kingdom. Jesus was overwhelmingly aware of the necessity of having a child's disposition to access the storehouse of heaven and the heart of the Father. Jesus was familiar with that all-dependent, trusting disposition, because He was once a child, just like all of us. But even as an adult He maintained complete reliance upon the Father, and He knows that we must do that, too. There was nothing He did or said that He did not attribute to the Father. Jesus reserved some of His harshest rebuke to those close to Him who dared to hinder the children who, by their very nature, possess prominence and preeminence in the plan of the kingdom.

Maybe the pastors today are the ones shooing away the requests and demands of the youth. Maybe the pastors today have relegated our students to nothing more than an after-thought or at best an annual youth weekend, but offer no weekly program of ministry and discipleship. "Suffer the children not!"

Jesus scolded. This could also be translated, "Don't hinder the youth!" Instead, we must prepare them and provide for them. In doing so, we endear them to the cross, and honor the disposition of the Savior towards children. If Jesus rebuked His beloved disciples because of their indifference shown towards the youth, what would He say of you and your commitment to the young of your congregation? What would Jesus say of you and your leadership after a quick canvass of your church's record of how youth ministry has been administered under your watch?

"On whose authority are you shutting the beaches down?" the mayor asked Chief Brody. "You can't just shut the beaches down, you need a resolution signed by the council."

Red tape. The chief wanted to prevent any further loss of life, while the mayor provided nothing but interference. Leadership ought to support the efforts of those who are concerned with the well-being of our youth, not oppose them.

Twenty years ago, I heard a pastor exhort words from his pulpit that still ring in my ears today. I had taken a youth ministry position in a church and opposition from the "powers that be" was clearly evident. My pastor recognized the internal red tape and the potential for destruction and one Sunday morning he declared from the front of the church, "We have worked so hard to get a youth minister, now that we have one, for God's sake let us not work against him."

He was my ally. The encouragement from his

unfettered support strengthened my resolve to be the best youth minister I could be. I was pleased to sit in his office and hear advice from his years of ministry. He regularly invited me to lunch, asked me to drive him on his ministry assignments, invited me to sit in his office and observe him pastor. I watched him make decisions and serve the flock. This great man of God, a pastor, leader, and mentor, invested mightily in me. His greatest investment was what he had the least of, time. He made time to approve me, critique me, and mentor me. Because I spent that time with him I saw him do his job well, and I learned how to love the youth I was charged to lead and pastor them with compassion. I leveraged any moment I spent with him, and considered it an advantage.

Do your ministers-in-training eagerly anticipate their time with you? Or is their time with you filled with intimidation, struggle, and frustration as they leave your office in quiet emptiness? You should be the one to rally support, grease the skids, generate resources to accommodate the courageous work of anyone who has the wherewithal to commit to serving your youth.

A recent Southern Baptist survey concluded that one year after high school graduation 88% of church-going youth will be missing from the radar screen of any worship experience. You have a very limited window to do what historically happens mainly between the ages of seven and eighteen. The percentage of people who become committed believers in Jesus after the age of eighteen is significantly low. The percentages drop drastically after the age of thirty-five. Most people who walk in a committed relationship with Jesus Christ first met and received him between the ages of seven and thirteen. The next largest group is between the ages of fourteen and eighteen. Consequently, it's our church-based youth programs that most desperately need focused attention to establish infrastructure, coordination, and funding.

On one assignment, my annual youth budget was $6,000. (After telling this story to youth workers many have sarcastically asked, "You had a budget?") During the preparation of the budget for the next year I was told by the church council that because of the church's financial hard times my budget was being cut to $3,600 and that I would have to fundraise to make up for my budget shortfall. We did car washes practically every weekend. We sold hats, calendars, t-shirts, and candy. We had to fund camps, retreats, conventions, lock-ins, and youth weekends. It was tough, but we made it. There were still things that our funding could not support, so we had to cut those from our program. The following year the church recovered financially. Instead of restoring our budget to $6,000, the budget committee concluded that since we did so well at $3,600 we would remain there. The church's annual budget was $500,000. The absolute best they could do for their youth was .72 percent of their annual budget. .72 percent is less than one percent of the church's annual budget and, sadly, is consistent with national averages.

Of every ministry population in the church, the youth are our most financially dependent. They need transportation, chaperones, and entrance fees to events and activities. Youth need to be fed, and they need guidance and structure. If funds are not available from the church to offset the cost of accommodating youth, the demand will fall on the parents. Why place additional financial burden on the parents and guardians who, in many cases, are struggling economically to sustain the family, and are already desperate for godly influence for their children? There are some families who can better support the work of ministry than others, but the church should own the responsibility to provide the funding foundation for a healthy youth ministry.

One year, I had the staff of my youth center on site at our community high school in southeast Washington, D.C. on the first day of school to offer assistance to the school's administration. While there, I had a shocking revelation. As I stood outside of the main entrance, I overheard extremly foul language coming from a young ninth grade student. I turned around and witnessed her frustration, bad behavior, and her state of ill-preparedness as she launched into her high school career. She had no backpack or school materials, she was not dressed in the school uniform, and was blatantly disrespectful to the staff. Suddenly I heard an adult woman call the girl's name with a loud and boisterous voice. It was her mom. A half-smoked cigarette hung from her mouth and she was extremely under-dressed (*everything* was hanging out). Instead of helping remedy the situation, she began to call the administration some names I hadn't even heard before. Her mouth was foul, her disposition disrespectful, and her presence rough and aggressive.

I realized in that moment that many of our youth are simply victims of adult failure. Granted, there are many hard-working, conscientious parents who do their absolute best to raise their children, often without the aid of a spouse. But, in many instances, youth are devoid of active and involved parents or guardians shaping their youthful pursuits. Many students have developed into who they are by no fault of their own, but rather as a result of premature and untrained parenting. They inherited generational dysfunction. There are some students who have perfect attendance not because they necessarily like school, they just don't like being at home. I know because I was one of those students.

My parents' fussing and fighting unnerved me. Their drinking and smoking disturbed me. School was where I found peace. But school can't offer eternal hope. School can prepare our students for the marketplace, but only a right relationship with Jesus Christ can prepare them for the human race, destiny, and for every tomorrow in their future.

But where, Pastor, does one discover this hope?

Not from the television or through a music media player. It's birthed from the consistent leadership of a youth minister and a comprehensive youth program designed to produce a kingdom-mentality and biblical worldview. Students need to develop a godly identity, established at a local church where outreach and discipleship to teens is thriving. Is that what's happening at your church? Is your church a safe haven for teens? Is the youth group growing under your leadership? Students who come to your church's youth group at least once will either never be seen again or they will come back and bring a friend. Which is it for you?

I was once asked by a reporter why I travel and speak to the youth of America and abroad as extensively as I do. The answer is simple. Most of the decisions that determine the quality of our adult life are made before the age of twenty-one. If students do not smoke before the age of twenty-one, statistics show tobacco use will not be an issue in their lives. If a student does not drink alcohol before the age of twenty-one, alcohol will probably not plague them as adults.

Scientists offer a biological explanation why patience and protection of your teens should be a pressing concern. Neurologist Frances Jensen says scientists used to think human brain development was pretty complete by age ten. The belief was that a teenage brain is just an adult brain with fewer miles on it. But we now know that isn't true.

Jensen states: "The largest part, the cortex, is divided into lobes that mature from back to front. The last section to connect is the frontal lobe, responsible for cognitive processes such as reasoning, planning, and judgment. Normally this mental merger is not completed until somewhere between ages 25 and 30."

This is the part of the brain that helps a person determine: *Is this a good idea? What is the consequence of this action?* It's not that teens don't have a frontal lobe, but they're going to access it more slowly.

That's because the nerve cells that connect teenagers' frontal lobes with the rest of their brains are sluggish. Teenagers don't have as much of the fatty coating called myelin, or white matter, that adults have in this area. Think of myelin as insulation on an electrical wire. Nerves need myelin for nerve signals to flow freely. Spotty or thin myelin leads to inefficient communication between one part of the brain and another. All of this is to say, our teens are deficient when it comes to quickly making the right decisions. I personally believe that Satan tries to exploit this deficiency.

The flesh, by nature, is impulsive. We must not only teach our teens what it means to live under the cross of Christ, we must help them put their faith into practice with practical application. If we don't, their young lives will be vulnerable to sabotage by the enemy. Neural insulation isn't complete until our mid-twenties. Pre-teens and teens need to be embraced with all the support we can offer.

Myelin deficiency is not the only big difference in a teenagers' brains. By nature, the brains of children and adolescents are more excitable. Their brain chemistry is tuned to be responsive to everything in their environment. After all, that's what makes kids able to learn new information so easily. But this can work in ways that are not so good. Consider the effects when a young brain learns to become addicted to alcohol (or nicotine, marijuana, cocaine, ecstasy).

Studies have shown that a teenager who smokes weed will still show cognitive deficits days later. An adult who smokes the same dose will return to a normal cognitive baseline much faster. Youth are different from young adults. One of the greatest mistakes a church can make is to group youth with the young adults. They are in two separate stratospheres! Young students are growing up too fast. Grouping them with young adults is like adding accelerant to a fire that's already out of control.

Youth are at severe risk and the pressure is on those of us who have a lamp. We better not hide it under a bush, but use it to lead the way.

Questions for reflection:

1. What are the concrete ways your church has made accommodations to serve your teens?

2. Do you think your church takes seriously into account the role of youth in God's divine plan for the building of the kingdom?

3. Young people are so utterly special to the God of this universe. Are they equally special to you?

If yes, can we verify your response by the structure of your children's and youth ministry? If no, why not?

4. If Jesus were to visit your church next week for a youth ministry audit, what changes would you make today before He comes?

Chapter 4
The Journey Begins

Let's travel back to Amity. The death of the Kitner boy prompted his mom to take matters into her own hands. Mrs. Kitner was not only distraught over the death of her son, she was also mortified that Chief Brody knew there was a shark feeding at the beaches in Amity, yet still allowed citizens in the water. She posted her own reward of $3,000 for the fisherman who could bring in the shark that viciously attacked and killed her boy. In passing the Chief at the pier, full of pain and disgust, she violently slapped the chief in the face.

"You knew!" she exclaimed.

For the youth minister handicapped by out-of-touch pastoral leadership, staring into the eyes of a frustrated parent who is desperate for help with her child is a numbing experience. The youth worker is committed to the students, but the limitations of a nonexistent budget, absentee supervisory support and direction, and the evaporation of human resources promotes "Mrs. Kitner-like" desperation.

Chief Brody recognized that obviously it was time to do something. Enter Quint. Brody convinces the mayor to hire Quint to kill the shark, and Brody and Hooper join Quint aboard *The Orca* to begin the hunt.

Remember my analogy of Quint as a representation of the head pastor or powers that be that can halt innovation and my reference to Brody as a youth pastor? Let's add Hooper to the mix as an example of a young volunteer called to assist the youth minister. Hooper, who is up on the latest technology, gets on Quint's boat with a number of advanced gadgets that he's used to study, catch, or immobilize sharks. They include spear guns with poison darts, a small metal cage, compressed air canisters for scuba diving, and more.

Quint's first reaction was notable; he laughed.

Pastor, have you ever thought your youth minister's requests to use the latest technology were unnecessary? Have you rolled your eyes when presented with a request to upgrade equipment or bring in new props to help get a message across to kids?

The fact of the matter is, these are desperate times calling for determined measures. The chart on the following page demonstrates just how true this is and paints a stark picture of what today's students face:

Top school discipline issues

1940s	1990s
Talking out of turn	Drug abuse
Chewing gum	Alcohol abuse
Making noise	Pregnancy
Running in the hall	Suicide
Cutting in line	Rape
Dress code violations	Robbery
Littering	Assault

Top ten problems as reported by U.S. students

Incident type	Number of Incidents	Percentage of Total Incidents Reported
1. Stress	910	15%
2. Bullying	588	10%
3. Depression	452	8%
4. Family Problems	257	4%
5. Fighting	216	4%
6. Peer Pressure	185	3%
7. Drugs	140	2%
8. Cheating on Schoolwork	116	2%
9. Cutting / Self-injury	108	2%
10. Suicide	107	2%

As reported by students enrolled in schools using AnComm's 'Talk About It®' anonymous online and text based reporting service. The annual AnComm 'Talk About It®' Report sample includes more than 70,000 students enrolled in 52 schools across 12 states.

The famous coach of the Green Bay Packers, the late Vince Lombardi, once said that he could win any football game with the same three offensive plays if every player executed his assignment with one hundred percent precision. One of those plays would have undoubtedly been the Green Bay Off Tackle Power Trap. It was introduced and extremely effective thirty years ago. What if it remained as Green Bay's main go-to play today? Today's defensive lineman are bigger than offensive linemen and faster than running backs. Defensive linebackers are even stronger than defensive lineman. Since Lombardi's time, opposing defenses have recognized the Off Tackle Power Trap and have adjusted their play to stop it, using stunts of their own.

If Green Bay kept executing that play, would the Off Tackle Power Trap still be as effective? No. Green Bay has had to change. Now you have the "reverse pivot, fake dive, quarter back triple option." Without change, there would be loss.

After "twenty years of catching sharks," Quint is content to take the same boat and use the same antiquated methods to catch this rogue, man-eating, two ton, great white shark. Sounds ridiculous, doesn't it? This wasn't the same old shark. It was much larger than anything that had come before. It was more determined and smarter than its predecessors. Hooper brought new ideas and methods. Chief Brody committed to use whatever worked. And Quint laughs at them.

I suppose my hypersensitivity to the plight of the

youth minister is the result of the countless conversations I have had with students throughout America who find themselves desperate for answers and hurting for God's unconditional love. Many students are simply unmotivated and unfulfilled with church youth groups. At one event, a student came to me long after the altar call and asked if I could pray for her. She was stuck in the self-destructive habit of cutting herself. I told her Jesus could help her to stop cutting herself.

"Have you asked Jesus into your life?" I asked.

She responded that she had not because her friends had not made the same decision. She was not willing to accept Jesus into her life because she was too afraid to do it alone. I have often wondered how many young men and women need the power of the risen Savior in their lives, but don't have an accommodating safe-haven of a relevant youth group to affirm their godly convictions.

At my youth center, a distraught eighteen year old came into my office.

"Steve, I need to talk," he said.

"What's the problem?" I responded.

He took a seat and burst into tears. I tried to calm him as he fought back his emotion.

"I lost my virginity last night," he confided. To be honest, I was initially somewhat relieved. I have had teens reveal much more tragic scenarios in the confines of my office. Not to trivialize the loss of virginity for an eighteen year old boy, but somehow I thought we could successfully process this disappointment and move forward. The young man continued.

"The person I lost my virginity with called me this morning and informed me that he is H.I.V. positive and that I should go get myself checked out."

I wasn't prepared for that addendum. Several issues were involved here. He was barely an adult and his partner was a twenty-nine year old man. Even with condom use, there remains a twenty-five percent chance the H.I.V. virus will spread from one infected partner to another. And because this virus is very clever, a positive result may not appear for as late as five to eleven years. So, once someone is exposed, testing should happen every six months for the next several years.

Fortunately we have the resources at our center to guide, counsel, direct, and support this young man as he enters adulthood. But do you see? We are not dealing with the same old shark. We must have a creative strategy, and comprehensive ministry to meet the demands of youth in crisis.

I had no idea I'd ever be a rapping preacher. But by God's providence, I launched into an effective rap ministry. Believe me it was not on my radar. Even today, I am not that much of a gospel rap fan. At one church's youth Sunday I petitioned God, "Lord, please don't make me rap here this morning." I could sense the disapproval of the "saints" in their cold stares.

God's response: "You must rap here today for two reasons. The youth here need some kind of identity with me. Secondly, there are some older believers that need to know that I am a whole lot bigger than they thought I was!"

At another church, on youth Sunday, I indicated that I was about to do a Christian rap song entitled *God is an Awesome God*. Several senior saints stood in disapproval, marched out of the church and stood just on the other side of the glass doors with folded arms noticeably demonstrating their disgust. They didn't realize that it was the same gospel rap that, when given in concert the night before, ushered several of their youth into the kingdom of God. In contrast to the reaction they gave me, when I called Rev. Ron Fowler, my hometown pastor, in 1983 from college to inform him of the new ministry tool God had added to my arsenal, his immediate response was, "When can you come home and perform your rap here?"

As Dean Jones, the late dean of the Howard University School of Divinity, always said, "The greatest challenge of the gospel is to find the appropriate metaphor!"

The gospel will always be the gospel. It will always be the virgin birth, the gruesome death, and the glorious resurrection of the risen Christ. Our challenge, as kingdom leaders, will always be, "How do we find the appropriate channel to make this gospel comprehensible to every population?" What will be the new device, analogy, ministry form, or resource, that may or may not even be discovered yet, that can assist the Holy Spirit to usher the next generation into the kingdom of God? The greater question is how will you respond when you encounter it? Will you fan the flame or put it out?

How did Quint respond to the great white shark?

"I'll get a barrel on him! He won't stay down long with a barrel on him!" Quint said.

Barrel dragging is an old technique used in shark hunting where the hunter seeks to harpoon the shark with a harpoon that has a line and a barrel attached to it. Under normal conditions, the shark drags the barrel until it becomes too exhausted to continue to evade the shark hunter. At that point the hunter would pull the shark in.

Chief Brody had already declared that the shark they hunted was over twenty-five feet long and weighed likely two tons. So ... a barrel? How absurd to base your strategy on what gave success thirty years ago. Brody said it best: "We need a bigger boat!" He was really saying: "We need a better paradigm! If the people of Amity deserve a fighting chance, Mr. Quint, please get a bigger boat!"

Pastor, the life of your church deserves a greater hope than the casual default hit or miss standard. When Chief Brody sighted the great white shark, Quint was able to harpoon it with a barrel. However, the shark uncharacteristically went underwater, mystifying Quint. *The Orca* began pursuit. This was no ordinary shark. Every approach taken by Quint to capture the shark was based on his ordinary past experiences.

While experience is a wise teacher, necessity is the

mother of invention. We are typically quick to rely on what has worked in the past. Whether it is a principle, technique, sermon, or joke. If it has previously garnered success, we confidently do it again or tell it again. We don't have that luxury when it comes to the tactics needed to defeat the enemy of our youth. Our old tactics don't faze the enemy. The venom of the dark side is decimating our youth and at best we barely win our youths' attention for an occasional seasonal special event.

"I've been catching sharks for twenty years," bragged Quint.

So what? It doesn't matter how many years you've been pastoring, the accomplishments you achieved "way back when" you were a youth minister, or how profound your Sunday sermons are from week to week. Woe to the leader who fails to mentor or provide for the young youth leader and equip him or her with the resources needed to build a comprehensive, effective, and relevant youth and/or children's program! The Sunday sermon applause you hear will be a regrettable consolation for a church whose movement turned into a monument because the next generation of members were not discipled as youth and the median age of the congregation is now the same as the pastor.

One evening, early in the hunt, Quint, Hooper, and the Chief share a drink in the hull of the ship and pass the time by comparing shark bites. It's a classic time of male bonding as they jockey back and forth to see whose shark bite is the largest and most gruesome.

Ultimately Quint and Hooper square off as they eagerly attempt to prove to one another "my bite is bigger than yours."

I've often wondered why we have in our human nature the drive to be bigger, better, or best in relation to our comparable peers. This distinction is particularly disconcerting when these same juvenile boastings seep into the fabric of our local 11 a.m. Sunday morning rituals.

"I don't need any volunteers, no mates, or too many captains!" Quint told the mayor before leaving the docks in Amity. Quint wanted all the responsibility, all of the expectations, and consequently all of the glory for the capture of the great white shark. "Me, me, me!" It was going to be his show. The truth is, Quint needed Chief Brody and Hooper regardless of who held the bragging rights for the largest shark bite.

I've seen that "me, me, me" disposition before. Why would a pastor of a church of seventy-five people, on a good Sunday, need a security team of fifteen men to usher him to the platform? There are some pastors who are so perpetually starved for attention, fame, and the spotlight they are unwilling to even share the church keys or the church office knowledge so that they remain the solution to all of the church's needs. This type of leader is unenlightened by the realization that a benchmark for success in leadership is not determined by how much knowledge and wisdom you "gather," but the degree to which you "scatter."

Dr. Myles Munroe put it best when he said, "Some

pastors chain themselves to their pulpits, lock themselves to their chairs and declare, 'This is my church, I'm never leaving this pastorate, this city or this job.'"

To respond to this, Dr. Munroe would say, "You are sick. You are a parasite." Anyone who makes this kind of declaration is simultaneously telling God that they are satisfied with all that they have attained and they are not available to go to the next level.

We need each other! Leaders need to work interdependently with junior leaders of the church to accomplish common goals. It's the essence of leadership. We see it in nature. The lion will not attack the elephant without the cooperation of the pride. The elephant welcomes the lion who is alone, and may even move towards him defiantly. That's why the lion will always summon the pride and identify the target so collectively they can execute the kill. Too many leaders are reluctant to empower others to join the hunt because they are unwilling for others to know that their way might work or they are disinclined to share the credit with anyone else when things go well.

Most youth workers are trying to get to the next level in relevancy, growth, and impact. To do so, they need pastoral leadership who are willing to work together to achieve youth ministry success. Dr. Myles Munroe has also said that one of the key qualifications for leadership is humility. The moment you say you have it (humility) you've just failed the test for leadership. Where are the pastors who could care less about who gets the credit or whose church is the biggest, better, or best? Where are the pastors who are, as Mary insisted at the wedding feast, willing to do whatever Jesus says to do, regardless of the risks involved? Where is the pastor that is so pouring into the staff a progressive vision for the continued success for their students and the future vitality of their congregation that he or she has confidently produced a viable successor? Too many pastors are in the hull of a doomed vessel comparing shark bites, oblivious to the circling predator that will one day sink the ship.

Questions for reflection:

1. When was the last time your youth minister asked for an upgrade in resources to bring his/her strategies more current? How did you respond?

2. How much time do you spend in deliberate mentorship with your youth minister (or staff person, or key volunteer)?

3. If your students were asked what problems they are currently facing, how do you think they would respond?

Chapter 5 | Shady Strategy

Quint employed the typically effective technique of barrel dragging as his core strategy to capture the great white shark. A shark's maximum striking force is great enough to pull a barrel under water for only a short period of time. The force a shark can generate in a continuous pull is insufficient to keep the barrel under water for long. The idea is to allow the shark to run until it becomes so exhausted that it cannot resist being pulled in by the hunter. The shark in *JAWS* ran with not one barrel on him, not two, but three barrels attached.

In addition, this shark was able to go under with three barrels on it for as long as it wanted. This behavior is completely unheard of among shark hunters. This shark was harpooned, shot by both a pistol and a rifle, had three barrels attached to it, yet it lived.

For our struggle is not against flesh and blood, but against the rulers, against the authorities, against the powers of this dark world and against the spiritual forces of evil in the heavenly realms. (Ephesians 6:12)

A major part of our defeat in youth ministry is the attempt of the church to "put a barrel on the shark." Leaders may have great intentions, yet they are fraught with poor strategy. The strategy to rescue our youth has been reduced to nothing more than a feeble, although sincere, attempt to distract and exhaust the shark with our gratuitous offensives.

"We may not have the thriving infrastructure of an established youth or children's ministry but we'll have a youth choir." Participation in the youth choir is helpful, but it is not enough.

"We may not be offering a powerful weekly youth event, but we'll annually pray over our students as we launch the school year." Bringing your students to the altar at the beginning of each school year for the laying on of hands is a powerful event. It's simply not enough.

"Our students may not have a yearly mission trip to demonstrate the power of service but we'll host a weak, shallow, and somewhat irrelevant Vacation Bible School for five days where only three of our core teens show up." Again, any participation in a vacation bible school event is significant. But it is a far cry from

the comprehensive strategy needed to defeat THIS shark.

While organizing a tour of school assemblies in a certain school district, I was pleased that only one out of thirteen schools opted out of our Drug Free Assembly Campaign. However, I wanted to know why the one school opted out. When we asked the principal for an explanation he confidently expounded, "We've had our drug talk already for the year."

I asked him if he saw the NFL playoffs the weekend before. He confirmed that he did. I asked how many beer commercials he saw. He estimated without hesitation that there were dozens! He, along with the students, experience a barrage of alcohol consumption messages in just one weekend of watching sporting events. And yet, he concludes that *one* counter-drug message a year is sufficient? Do you see that the strategy is suspect? We are dealing with a shark that can run and go under with three barrels on it. This is a spiritual battle! This is war! We must employ every possible resource to gain the victory here, not simply add more barrels in a half-hearted attempt to solve our problem.

For though we live in the world, we do not wage war as the world does. The weapons we fight with are not the weapons of the world. On the contrary, they have divine power to demolish strongholds. We demolish arguments and every pretension that sets itself up against the knowledge of God, and we take captive every thought to make it obedient to Christ. (2 Corinthians 10:3-5)

How long will we continue to be convinced that our efforts to serve our youth are merely good enough? Good enough is never good enough when God's standard demands the very best. I shudder to think what life would be like if Jesus avoided the cross and the crucifixion because He was convinced that the beatings he endured were "good enough."

The language in 2 Corinthians 10:3-5 is dynamic. **Wage** war, weapons we **fight** with, **demolish** strongholds, **demolish** arguments, **take** captive! Are these words and phrases that describe the activity of youth ministry at your church? Yes, doing something is better than doing nothing, but don't your youth deserve more than "just something?"

With smoke and mirrors we appease our congregants with long explanations and crafty phrases that give the appearance effective youth ministry is existent. But any careful closer look will reveal the sad reality. Credible and intentional ministry to our youth is woefully deficient. Students harbor much uncertainty about their lives and their future. They are sheep waiting for a shepherd to lead them, all while the wolves gather about. The field is ready for the harvest! It's the obligation of the pastor to identify a leader and equip that leader so that the pretensions and arguments that are set against the youth can be demolished. Other translations say in the 2 Corinthians verses that we are to **conquer**, **overthrow**, and **bring** into captivity speculations, imaginations, and lofty opinions. Get it out of your head that we are to weaken, exhaust, or slow down the enemy. His work must be demolished! We don't hinder, wear out, or get control of the flesh. The flesh has but one discourse, it must die!

    As an undersized outside linebacker on a Division-I college football team, I relied heavily on perfecting and employing my defensive techniques. At only six-feet-tall, two hundred pounds, I found myself lined up across from tight ends as tall as six-feet-five inches and weighing up to two hundred sixty-five pounds or heavier. When the running back came my way, my tendency was to hit and engage the tight end directly in front of me and quickly look past that tight end in an attempt to make the tackle. In doing so, I'd miss the tackle every time. The tight end would keep me tied up just enough to prevent me from making the play. In time and with practice I learned how to hit, engage, and escape the tight end and his block first, then freely make the tackle on the ball carrier coming my way. Similarly, pastors play "footsie" with the enemy too often when it comes to the needs of their youth program. Too many are perfectly comfortable waiting for a volunteer to offer a shell of a youth program that won't cost the church any money. In the end you get what you pay for. Lethargy keeps you tied up just enough to prevent you from ever securing the victory. As a consequence, a meaningful and full-fledged ministry to youth, whether two, twenty, or two hundred students, is never developed. Whatever diversion keeps you from executing a plan that rectifies your church's fledgling and suffering youth ministry efforts must be outright destroyed, so that the greatest good can be birthed in your students.

Another strategy Quint used was to attempt to drag the shark into the shallow waters and drown him. When I first heard Quint offer this tactic in the movie I thought it was not possible.

"Can a shark really drown?" I asked myself. Point of fact, some species can drown because they need to swim constantly in a certain motion in order to breathe. If you drag the shark back and forth it can drown! When a shark swims, they have to move in a wave-like motion. This helps push the water into their gills, which pull the oxygen from the water. Once they stop moving, or if they are forced into a backwards motion, the shark gets no oxygen and its lungs fill with water. So it was a plausible approach for Quint to suggest in normal situations. But let us remember, they already knew there was nothing normal about this hunt or this shark.

I have a colleague who works with students at an elementary school in Washington, D.C. In this school, in one class, many of the students have probation officers. Any guess what grade? First! First graders have probation officers and no, this is not normal. About 135,000 teens will bring a gun to school every day in America. Normal? Every day in America, approximately 2,463 children are victims of abuse or neglect. Normal? In just one year (2003), 2,827 children and teens died from gun violence. This is more than the number of fighting American men and women killed in hostile action in Iraq in the three-year period of 2003 to April 2006. Normal? From 1979 to 2003, firearms killed approximately 100,000 children and teens. Children are twice as likely as adults to be victims of violence and more likely to be killed by adults than by other children. I ask again: Is this normal?

So what happens when outdated, antiquated, and disconnected strategies are applied in these battles? What happens when faced with a robust, determined enemy? Quint found out quickly. In his arrogant attempt to drag the shark into the shallows, the engine on *The Orca*, his ill-equipped fishing vessel, burned out and the shark remarkably towed the boat away from the shores and into the deep waters. Quint and his crew became the victims of a flawed strategy and visionless leadership.

Without vision, people perish. The word of God is certain and clear on this point. Where there is no leader defining the way, or prophet expounding the law, or no priest to teach the knowledge of the Lord, and where there is no vision, the people will perish. I find it interesting that Proverbs 29:18 falls on the heels of a discussion about how parents ought to discipline their children that they may give their parents peace. The verse reads: "Where there is no vision, the people perish: but he that keepeth the law, happy is he." (KJV)

It's time for leaders to ante up! Let's present our vision for the sake of our children and the future of our families! The global strategy for establishing peaceful nations begins in the homes where parents speak the vision. In the homes where the family has disintegrated and leadership struggles, the vision must come from God to the head of the house. The head of the family needs you, Pastor, to be the covering and to inspire vision by example.

The shark is now towing *The Orca*. The crew is at odds about strategy, there is no vision, and the engine burns out! Burnout! How many times have you witnessed burnout? How many times have you seen an overworked and underpaid youth worker sitting across from your desk, requesting to be relieved of his assignment? The average lifespan of a youth minister in any one place is about eighteen months. In the beginning, the youth minister has a vision for the youth of his or her community. Then, the stress of operating within an inadequate budget and in an environment of subordination compels the youth worker to find viable ways to raise funds to finance his vision of ministry. But, having to curtail that vision because the fund raising doesn't produce the money needed to support the vision, takes the wind out of the sails of a youth worker who is sincerely trying to make a difference. When this scenario is repeated time after disappointing time, burnout is inevitable.

Feeling outmatched by the shark and desperate to survive, Chief Brody makes another attempt to radio for a bigger boat. Quint, in response, violently smashes the radio with a bat. Chief Brody explodes in toxic frustration.

"You are certifiable, Quint you know that? Certifiable!" the chief screams.

Hooper also tried to get Quint to slow down. "You are putting too much stress on the engine!" he assailed.

But there was no getting through to Quint. He went from one extreme to the next. He pushed it full-throttle. Then it happened. Burnout! The engine blew, sparks flew, and fire ensued. A frantic dash to the fire extinguisher silenced the fire, but the damage was done. Haughtiness comes before a fall. Pride left *The Orca* stranded. That's where many of our churches' youth programs are ... stranded.

The evidence is clear, you just may not have had the courage to admit it. Youth ministry is neither moving forward or backward. It's simply stuck, drifting from week to week, year to year, unchanged, unmotivated, and uninteresting. There is no vision, no dream, and the people, the children, are perishing. Who do you suppose God will hold accountable for this condition? Whatever state your youth ministry is in today, it's there ultimately as a result of leadership, good or bad. You may have a core group of students who show up every time the doors of the church are open, but what about the multitude of youth who are what I call "present but not accounted for?" They are present because grandma, mom, auntie, and uncle still attend the church. They are not accounted for and do not show up because age-relevant ministry is not available. What about the youth across the street from the church on the playground or the teenagers down the street hanging out at the park? What about the overlooked mission field called a high school that sits in the backyard of the church?

For many pastors, the strategy to reach lost youth is devoid of the teeth it takes to make a real difference in these places. In some cases, it is because the pastor is surrounded by silent voices that decry his egotism and hard-headedness yet do not have the courage to speak aloud. His own ears have become deaf to the need for change by years of his own success, doing things his own way, in his own style. Or maybe even it's simply a matter that he is uninformed of the dearth of the church youth. Whether it's the Mega Holy Church of The Father or Wee Little Church on the Prairie, this disease is not prejudiced.

Back to *The Orca*. The engine is blown, the vessel is taking on water, the shark (with three barrels on it) has towed the boat back to the deep. It's only when their fate seems sealed that Quint passes out the life jackets. In the face of this frightening turn of events Quint asks Hooper rather ashamedly, "What can some of these things you've brought on board do?"

The timing of this question is preposterous. Quint knows that if they end up in the water, the shark wins. Hooper must have thought, "With the boat sinking, and no way to radio for help, and life jackets distributed, NOW you ask me how my expertise can save us? The same expertise that could only illicit a hearty laugh when I boarded the boat? *Now* you show interest?" Hooper suffered through all of Quint's early ridicule. And just when their doom was imminent, only then Quint is humbled to invite assistance.

Tragedy strikes your church family. A stray bullet takes one of your own. A thirteen year old son of a prominent active member takes his own life. One of your brightest stars has lost her light too soon because she was driving drunk. For years you've gotten away with only a modest investment in your church's youth. Despite being in a neighborhood full of students, for twenty years you have barely managed to get more than the same ten to attend a paltry Friday night youth meeting. Now, when hope is all but gone and a cadre of parents are knocking at your door, the deficiency is clear to everyone. NOW you want to meet with the youth leader? After years of inactivity, and laughing at his or her proposed radical means and methods, *now* you inquire about change? After categorically vetoing any cutting edge idea that didn't originate with you, and after putting out the fire of spirit-led innovation, *now* you want to talk it over? With only twenty and a half students from your church of three thousand (twenty teens, but one brings his little brother, the half, because mom says it's a package deal) showing up for a youth activity you, out of desperation, *now* ask, "What is this thing called gospel rap?" Or you say, "Tell me again how a Friday night skate park would work?"

It's amazing to me that when the boat was

sinking, Quint finally opened his mind to other strategies. Is that you, Pastor? Do you face the embarrassment of possessing the potential and capability to do "greater things than these," as Jesus promised, but the lack of a fruitful ministry to youth unmistakably reveals years of neglect?

If so, I have one word: Repent.

How did Jesus respond to that fig tree that withheld its fruit? Jesus expects not only that we produce fruit in our personal spiritual lives, He's anticipating that which we steward to yield fruitful, righteous benefit to the body of believers! As you examine the state of your ministry to the youth you oversee, you must honestly ask, "If Christ passed by, would He be blessed by the fruit or would He curse this tree?"

Hooper had a metal cage and a tranquilizer among his equipment. He promised that if he were lowered into the water and had the right opportunity, he could shoot the tranquilizer into the mouth of the shark and paralyze him. It was a good strategy and, even though it ended up not being the right strategy, at least it got them pushing the envelope. At least it was a "falling forward" strategy. It was progressive, risky, and daring. It failed, but what if the boat was healthy and it was still early in the hunt? What if time, energy, and resources were not wasted trying out the "barrel" thing? What if Quint, Hooper, and Chief Brody all had wetsuits, scuba gear, and tranquilizing guns? What if they had been able to triangulate the shark, bait him with the cage, and fire high-powered tranquilizing darts into his mouth and torso? Well, there would be no movie.

Are you in search of a feasible strategy? True visionary leaders never lead alone. They incorporate the support of the team and empower others to contribute to accomplishing a common goal. As referenced earlier, once a lion identifies its prey, he summons the pride by making a low frequency grunting noise. Lionesses recognize the grunting, circle the target, and strategically pounce while the male lion watches. His role is to ensure the lionesses are safe while they attack. He looks on, along with the cubs, but they all enjoy the benefits of the kill.

Cooperation and support for what is important allows time for ideas and strategy to be developed in context with all available information. Without cooperation, the urgent becomes the priority, and the important is undeveloped. Fear-laced schemes that lack the necessary time to be fully vetted are launched into action. They cause more harm than good and leave behind the fragments of another youth worker and his vision in the wake of a vessel headed nowhere. Instead of vision and then action, you have action without vision. Vision without action is a daydream. But action without vision is a nightmare.

Questions for reflection:

1. What are the barrel-dragging strategies (i.e. antiquated) currently in place within your youth program?

2. Have you witnessed signs of burnout in your youth staff? In what ways?

3. What do you do currently to intentionally avoid burn-out among all your staff, particularly your youth workers?

4. What can you begin to do, this month, to take solid steps to preventing your youth staff from burnout?

Chapter 6 | The Super Hero

Students are arguably the most difficult population of people to reach, win, and disciple. Students are unpredictable, excitable, at-risk, bold, different, a little crazy, funny, fighting, eager, inquisitive, in (puppy) love, angry, hurt, alone, curious, hungry, broke, and emotional–often all at the same time! And, they are worthy of our time.

God, in His infinite wisdom, breathes into the DNA of certain individuals a life mission to serve these students. It's too bad that the only way to minister to these peculiar people is for one to have an unlimited budget, lots of volunteers, strong pastoral support, a congregation that's got your back, a competitive salary, plenty of designated space, parents who help but never get in the way, one or two paid staff, and plenty of vacation time! Certainly I am only jesting here. I do believe, however, that in many instances youth workers are expected to be super heroes and heroines. We ask them to raise their own budget, recruit and train volunteers, inform and coordinate the parents, plan, prepare, promote, and perform the ministry, largely without any of the tongue in cheek needs in place listed above.

Most youth ministers enter their first assignment untrained and equipped with only a godly passion to fulfill a call they barely understand. At one of my first youth ministry assignments I worked part-time for $12,000 annually while simultaneously working full-time at another youth-related job. I realize the salary alone puts me far ahead of the game as far as local youth ministry goes. It was this church's first paid youth ministry position in its history.

Of course I say I worked "part-time," but I have come to realize that no such animal exists. With the limited help of an unpaid co-leader, our weekly youth event looked like this: Each Friday I'd pick up the church van (which was a 20 minute drive across town). Then, at around 5:30 p.m., I'd begin picking up students who needed a ride. We'd arrive at the church for our 7:30 p.m. youth meeting, barely in time to set up. I would then execute the planned youth ministry event/meeting. My helper would prepare and provide some sort of snack for fellowship afterwards. Then, per the church's request and because it was a shared space, we'd have to clean up and prepare the area for its next use. I then waited for the parents who could come pick up their kids to do so, before loading the van with the remaining students and driving them home. I would then gas up the van and return it to the cross-town residence of the church van driver, where I had picked it up earlier that day. I would then get in my car and drive the forty miles to my home from the church.

On average I got home between 1:00 and 1:30 a.m. every Friday night. My marriage was young and my first child was under a year old. Both my marriage and my ministry were fragile. I had an immense passion to impact the young lives entrusted to me and to satisfy the pastor who, contrary to the recommendation of the youth minister search committee, appointed me for this inaugural position. I was burning the candle at both ends, learning a new full-time job while simultaneously serving part-time on my first paid youth ministry assignment.

All this took place in a city under siege that, at that time, was nicknamed the "murder capitol of the nation." We had already buried one thirteen year old girl from our church community and it wouldn't be long before another one of our teens would be sent away for good, serving a double-life sentence, convicted of first degree murder and first degree attempted murder. I thought that if I could just get someone else to drive the van, it would make my assignment so much more feasible. If not a van driving volunteer, I thought if I could just get someone to set up and break down before and after our weekly Friday night event, I could probably spend more time ministering to the youth.

The Youth Council (YC) asked how my new assignment was going. The YC was comprised of the pastor, a few parents, my supervisor, and a few others. I responded by citing our rise in numbers, ministry successes, and projected goals.

"Is there anything you need from us?" the pastor asked.

I quickly outlined my Friday night routine and said, "I could use some help." I couldn't hide the exasperation in my voice.

In response to my plea, a council member quickly interjected, "Isn't that what we are paying you for?"

Don't get me wrong, I know that's what I was paid to do, it's just that the twenty hours per week I was expected to put in typically turned into thirty hours a week. Coupled with a full-time job requiring forty hours a week, one could easily see why attempting to satisfy this dual role one would require a superhero's cape along with superpowers to go with it. I found out how difficult it was to keep a part-time youth ministry position to truly part-time hours. When I wasn't with the youth, I was thinking about them. When not thinking about the youth, I was thinking of ways to expand and strengthen the ministry. Youth ministry is not merely a one-weeknight experience.

Truly effective ministry includes Sunday school, campus visits, phone calls, volunteer recruitment, fund raising, ministry planning, counseling calls, and more. When I was told by the YC, "Isn't that what we are paying you for?" I actually heard, "You are on your own buddy, suck it up, get it done, whatever your personal expense may be."

I was spending so many hours away from my home that if I got home and my wife and daughter were out I literally found myself checking the refrigerator door expecting to find a note saying, "I can't take it anymore, Nicole (our infant daughter) and I have left you!"

I'll never forget reading an article posted in a Christian publication titled *Why I Left My Husband*. The wife said that her husband was a great man, a wonderful Christian, and a powerful youth minister. She went on to detail how he grew the youth ministry by twenty-five percent in his first year and had similar growth his second and third years. She said that when he was not with the youth, he was thinking about them. Her words I read that day made a permanent impression in my mind. She said, "My husband gave his job one hundred percent, that's why I left him. There's not much left after one hundred percent."

When Chief Brody prepared to join Quint and Hooper on *The Orca* for this epic adventure, he struggled to say goodbye to his wife on the pier. The chief understood the risks involved and knew he possibly might not return. His commitment to the lives of the people of Amity, who he was sworn to protect and serve, was greater than his fear of the unknown. Mrs. Brody was well aware of the butchery of which the shark was capable. She also knew her husband had an uncommon fear of the water that could be all but paralyzing for him. She was forced to accept the risks that accompanied the chief's position, including the risk of loss of his life.

During their anxious, yet tender, farewell Quint boisterously interrupts with a harsh interjection, "Come on chief, daylight's burning, say goodbye. We've got to get going!"

Quint's myopic view of his selfish agenda blinded him to the stress of husband and father weighted by the fears and expectations of the people of Amity. On the boat, it was not only the chief of Amity radioing for a bigger boat; it was a family man who was loved by others. In my meeting with the YC, it was not merely a young youth minister saying he needed help, but a husband and father.

Those who choose to minister the word and doctrine to youth deserve some degree of comfortable maintenance and relief. The Scripture says, "Do not muzzle an ox while it is treading out the grain." (Deuteronomy 25:4) In ancient times, an animal was used to spin a wheel or walk a threshing floor to separate the wheat from the stalk/chaff. Those who were first to harness animal power to thresh wheat quickly discovered that their "power source" was eating the grain they were harvesting. Animal owners quickly began to muzzle the ox/donkey to keep it from eating the grain. In the Old Testament Law, God commanded Israel to permit the animal doing the labor to share in the benefits of its hard work. This principle is designed to teach us that those who work hard to produce ought rightly to share in the benefits of their production.

This notion of "not muzzling the ox" must be important because it's referenced twice in the New Testament. The first interpretation views this passage as a proverbial saying, not really applicable to an ox, but showing concern for the laborer and his wages. The second interpretation focuses on the humanitarian character of the law: the concern is for the care of the animal. For the purposes of this analogy, I will emphasize the second interpretation. Show concern and care for the animal, or in our discussion, the laborer we call "youth minister."

Quint wanted all of the money and showed neither care nor concern for the chief. Not only did Quint break up what in all likelihood could have been a man's final moments with his wife and soul mate, he later dismissed Mrs. Brody's call when she reached out to her husband by radio. I can only imagine the encouragement and support the chief would have felt if given the chance to talk to his bride in the midst of this frightful ordeal. Quint didn't allow it.

"Hello Mrs. Brody. The chief is fine, we're doing a little fishing, be home by dinner, over and out!" Quint blurted across the radio to Mrs. Brody before quickly hanging up.

I am shocked when I encounter a pastor or church leadership who routinely treat the life and family of their youth minister with the same disregard. When I was a young youth minister, I needed all of the input, direction, care, and concern I could find. I was still discovering the dynamics of "husband and wife" when the challenge of parenting was thrown into the mix. I found myself struggling to financially support my young family when there seemed to consistently be more month at the end of the money.

Feverishly trying to process the passion of my call to serve the youth of my church as their ambassador, confidant, youth pastor, and counselor placed a demand on any and all reserves of my energy each week. Negotiating significant demands, with limited resources, produced toxic levels of stress that were detrimental to me physically, spiritually, and emotionally. While it is true that God does not put more on us than we can bear, sometimes we place more on each other than is right. Are you placing undue burden on your youth minister?

The tipping point can prove disastrous.

I discovered this firsthand one hot June night, while on retreat with my students. It was my first Father's Day weekend. Instead of spending it with my wife and infant daughter, I was meeting thirty students and their parents in the church parking lot before heading to Covenant Village Camp for a weekend youth retreat. It was the only summer weekend possible to host this first retreat. Starting at the beginning of the day we were to leave, one by one, each of my five volunteers contacted me and reneged on their commitment to serve. My last volunteer gave notice to the church office that they would not be attending, forty-five minutes before our church parking lot rendezvous. I was all alone. I frantically searched my Rolodex for at least one female adult who could help me for the weekend. With the students growing more anxious and the parents growing impatient, I was on the brink of canceling the event. At the last moment, I found the person I needed. (The fact that one parent disapproved of the volunteer because her daughter and this volunteer didn't "get along" almost sabotaged the whole weekend. But that is a story for another time.)

After a two-hour drive we arrived at the camp. My strength was already depleted. I was already over-exhausted. Conflict arose on the second night. One student pushed back one time too many while I was giving instructions to a group of disrespectful boys. A beefy young man, bigger than most fifteen-year-olds, tried to walk away while I was speaking. I stopped his movement by quickly grabbing his arm, insisting that he not walk away while I was speaking. To this he defiantly responded, "You better take your hands off of me." I reached my breaking point.

Images of my wife and daughter, home alone on Father's Day weekend, where I wanted to be, flashed through my mind. I was sleepy, tired, leading alone, and running on fumes. I was making something out of nothing on a retreat without the support or budget I needed to succeed. Fresh out of the NFL, two hundred twenty pounds of a grown man, I had a fifteen-year-old kid, whose mom I begged to allow him to come on the retreat, telling me "I'd better take my hands off of him."

With all of my might I reached back to swing as hard and violently as possible to smack this young kid! I swung forward while simultaneously releasing a loud, deep, guttural scream. At the last second, as my punch came towards his forehead, I purposely missed by no more than inches and with an open hand I turned and hit the top right corner of the door in the entryway where I stood. That was the grace of God. I hit that door with such force I ripped the door completely off its hinges. I then forearmed the chest of drawers at my right side with a linebacker-style shiver. That hit carried such power that the entire piece of furniture crumpled into a pile of wood on the floor. And finally, with my left forearm, I did the same another piece of bedroom furniture, garnering the same result. I cried with a loud voice, "I DON'T HAVE TO BE HERE!"

Then I buckled to the floor in tears. The palm of my right hand with which I had struck the door was split wide open with a four-inch gash. The room was deathly silent. No one moved. A few of the students began to cry because they had never seen Steve, their youth pastor, in such a state. My hand still bears a lifelong scar from that day over twenty years ago. Judging from the damage to the door, if I had struck the boy instead, he would have suffered permanent damage or even worse, he could have died. My work in ministry would have been aborted before it ever had a chance to truly begin.

I am not a superhero. Neither are your youth workers. They are ordinary people with an extraordinary call on their lives to build healthy relationships with youth that will help shape them into the young adult men and women of God they are destined to become.

Youth service workers in para-church youth service organizations are no exception to these principles. A colleague, who is a former pro-athlete and gifted speaker, described to me his monthly assignment as a speaker for his organization. He was away from home for thirteen consecutive days, off the road for a week, then back on the road for ten days.

"You have got to be kidding me," I exclaimed! "There is no way a Christian organization could make that kind of request on the time of a family man with young children at home, and maintain a clear conscience."

Those gifted individuals who serve youth, whether in schools or the local churches, require a pastor who is allied to protect the emotional and family health of that individual.

A few colleagues and I started a group called the Washington Youth Network. It was a vehicle for youth service providers to gather on a regular basis for networking and encouragement. In one meeting a young woman raised her hand to share a thought. When called upon she began to speak, but struggled to fight back the tears. She was the youth minister at her small church and had a burning call to make a difference. She began to sob uncontrollably. Between her gasps she revealed the source of her pain.

"I have no support! I'm alone. The pastor doesn't support me. It seems like no one cares."

She was an ox that was muzzled at her church. Is there an ox muzzled at yours? Are you withholding wages?

I was once asked to speak at a church youth weekend event. It was early in my speaking and preaching ministry. The fee for each session was $300. That included three talks: one Friday, Saturday, and Sunday morning for a total of $900.

The youth minister told my office, "We really want Steve to come and empower our youth but we can't afford the fee." So we reduced the fee to $100 per session.

"We don't have that much either," the youth minister replied. Resources have never prevented me from taking any ministry assignment. Sometimes I'd just like to see how committed the church is to their youth. Besides, I'm going to prepare as if there is no Holy Spirit, and preach with nothing but the Holy Spirit regardless of the fee. In this instance, we were actually one year away from the Youth Weekend in question.

My office asked the youth minister a question, "Since we have a year before the event, do you think the youth group can do a fundraiser between now and next year to raise the $300?" my staff asked.

"We are in a building program, and the pastor said that any group that does a fundraiser has to give the money to the building program," the youth minister said.

My heart sank when I heard that report. For this pastor, the church building program was more important than the youth group bringing in a youth communicator to empower their students for three nights, and for only $300. I accepted the assignment.

Because of poor planning, they were forced to cancel Saturday night and the Sunday morning youth service. I presented to their youth on Friday night, they paid me $100 and I donated it back to the youth group. They needed it more than I did.

The stories are countless of the youth worker slighted by the pastor when it comes to compensation, care, and concern. One church had a youth minister who was one of the most talented and gifted I had seen. I couldn't believe that a church this progressive had no stipend or salary for this outstanding young man. He had a small family and drove a gas-guzzling vehicle. I asked him if his church could at least help him out each month on his gas expenses.

"It's not in the budget," he was told.

This was another example of the expectation of superhero exploits to manifest in the form of a humble servant obeying God's call. The expectations don't change. We expect the youth minister/counselor to fulfill the pastor's and parents' demands like Superman with limited or no support or finances. Language that compels volunteers to join the ministry to the youth needs to come from the pulpit. Church leadership needs to be the champions that solicit the resources needed to sustain the funding targets for the youth ministry. The Church at large is desperate today for pastoral leadership that possesses strong convictions of the divine mandate to steward comprehensive and successful ministry to our youth.

Questions for reflection:

1. Is there an example of a youth event that had to be canceled at your church due to lack of resources or poor planning?

2. Upon reflection, is the reason the event failed on account of the youth worker being "muzzled"? Is there something you, as pastor, could have done to help?

3. Who is expected to wear the superhero's cape in your church? What plans are in place to protect the home life and well-being of that individual? (Or those individuals?)

Chapter 7 Hooper Brings the Edge

Hooper, the marine scientist, had specific expertise in tracking, studying, and successfully capturing sharks. He explained to the others how, as a young teen, a shark took a bite out of his tiny boat. From that moment on, he dedicated his life to the study of sharks. He studied their feeding habits, mating rituals, and communication styles. He knew their normal and abnormal activities. Hooper invested in the newest, most advanced tools and equipment to make his work successful. He brought many of these things aboard *The Orca*. This was no pleasure cruise for Hooper. He knew the challenge they embarked on was immense and carried deadly risks. Hooper's keen understanding of his subject facilitated his commitment to leave no stone unturned in preparation. In the short time he met and dined with Chief Brody, and from his brief exposure to Quint, it was clear to him that they were going to need all of the help they could get. Hunting and destroying this man-eating shark required a collaborative effort. Hooper knew it, and jumped right into the foray upon arrival.

Remember, a bounty had been placed on the capture and or killing of the shark by the bereft Mrs. Kitner. On that first day, dozens of novices headed out in rowboats, sail boats, and small fishing vessels to try their hand at winning the $3,000 reward. They used dynamite, chum lines, and all kinds of strange lures to capture a shark that they had no idea was larger than many of their vessels. It was pure chaos, and by that day's end, a shark was captured. The mayor was quick to identify it as "the" shark they were looking for.

After a late night, unofficial autopsy, Hooper realized that it was actually not the right shark. Hooper witnessed the mayor's ignorance and the lack of support the chief got from Amity's town executives. Hooper also seemed well aware of Chief Brody's weaknesses and was eager to assist this sincere police chief in capturing the shark. Because of Hooper's expertise, his opinion and perspective were different from the others. He was more informed and mostly accurate.

When they first met, Quint grabbed Hooper's hands. He rubbed them, doing an unscientific examination of Hooper's sea-worthiness. Noting their smooth, unmarked and unscathed texture, Quint dismissed Hooper as a "city boy" with nothing valuable to offer him. He disqualified Hooper's training and expertise based on his own crude test. Quint drew a quick conclusion of whether or not Hooper had anything worthwhile to contribute to this mission. Quint decided he needed neither Hooper's city boy expertise nor his shiny fancy equipment to catch this shark.

It's amazing the things we cannot see when we are blinded by our own preconceived notions and when we are prejudiced by our own experiences. Radical times call for radical measures. Believe me, we live in very radical times for the youth of this generation. It's the foolish man who does not employ the wisdom of wise counselors. One of the most dangerous places for a pastor to dwell is in the valley of "I know it all." It's when we are convinced that our way is best, our plan is best, our approach is best, and our resolution is best that we forfeit the greatest good. The youth worker likely does not possess the experience of the pastor. But if he or she is anointed by God to serve the youth, who is to say his or her perspective and critical thinking are not assets that should be taken seriously?

As I travel among youth populations throughout America I always glean new insights, norms, and vernacular from students that I incorporate into fresh strategies to reach more lost youth. Even though I have years of experience and nationally noted successes I am more than aware that I still need all the help I can get!

Using the information I gather always pays off in instant credibility. Credibility (or "cred" to the youth) is a necessity for anyone attempting to access their world. A popular trend with successful companies is to offer employees financial rewards for ideas that would improve the company's efficiency. Top management knows that employees who are in the field doing the work or at the workstation answering the phones have the greatest inclination to nuances, that, if deployed, would enable the company to move forward faster and more efficiently. In many cases, if the employee's recommendation is used, cash rewards can get into the hundreds of dollars. In the marketplace there are a number of characteristics that differentiate companies who, as Jim Collins writes in *Good to Great*, go from being good companies to being great companies.

Collins' research team completed a five-year project to determine what it takes to change a good company into a great one. They systematically scoured a list of 1,435 established companies to find every extraordinary case that made a leap from no-better-than-average results to great results. How great? To qualify for "great" status, a company had to generate cumulative stock returns that exceeded the general stock market at least three times over fifteen years—and it had to be a leap independent of its industry.

One characteristic of a company who crosses the good to great bridge is that they employ the "who first then what" philosophy. Companies that go from good to great must invest in the right people for the move forward before attempting to move at all. In other words, you need both the expertise of Mr. Hooper and the passion of Chief Brody to be successful. And to catch the shark, Hooper, Quint, and Chief Brody must blend their talents in the right mix to accomplish their goal.

I believe in every church there is a remnant of people who have all of the necessary ingredients to build and sustain a viable youth ministry. Who first, then what! I am astonished at the length to which a church will go in the "what" category before investing in the "who." The finances for the youth center, the research of popular youth ministry trends, and the teen curriculum or strategy all may establish the "what," yet it's the anointed and gifted "who" that will determine true success. You, Pastor, must drive, support, and fund this effort. Tragically this desired framework rarely exists because the "Chief Brodys" are rarely identified or supported and the "Hoopers" are rarely respected or they are simply written off as unnecessary.

Because of the success I've had, I am occasionally asked where I received my training to engage and address the youth of America the way I do. I've had no formal training on presentation styles. I've been enrolled in the school of the Holy Spirit, where I remain a life-long student. As I research, study, observe, and build healthy relationships with young people, God deposits in me ideas, illustrations, antidotes, and techniques that I employ through the lens of contemporary teenage culture. I dump my skill set into the lap of the God of the universe and then let go with fire. It's what I've been called to do. And yes, I have had success. Not incidental success but long-term success that has spanned more than twenty years.

I tell you, there is someone in your church with this same passion for youth and the same skill set, albeit uncultivated. As you read this book, know that they already have what's needed to build success with the youth ministry of your church. Pastors need to, as Paul exhorted Timothy, "fan the flame" (2 Timothy 1:6). Pastor, fan the flame of the youth worker in your midst. You know who they are because they are always coming to you to talk about the youth. Don't be fooled by their appearance. Man looks on the outside, but God examines the heart. God has already written in their DNA the gift to lead and impact the youth of your church and community. They are desperate for your support, encouragement, and direction. Facilitate it! Take the high road! Humbly avail yourself and use your influence as an unconditional resource to help this person build a team and a strategy to reach your youth.

I find it remarkable in the movie *JAWS* how Hooper exhibited his expansive knowledge of sharks. He was quickly able to characterize the size of the shark in question with nothing more than a cursory examination of the bite marks on the first victim. Hooper identified the origin of the shark first captured by the smell of its insides during the autopsy. After holding a shark tooth in his hand that he had removed from the sunken vessel of a missing fisherman, Hooper deduced that the shark they were seeking was definitely a Great White. My, what extraordinary familiarity and knowledge of sharks Hooper carried.

Quint forfeited the use of this expertise. Quint squandered Hooper's resourcefulness to the team, preferring instead to trust his untrained, obsolete, rusted skill set. If the shark were caught his way then the credit, the glory, and the acknowledgement would all be his. There was no doubt Quint experienced this kind of success and glory before. His boathouse was adorned with mountings of past catches, humongous jawbones, and taxidermal trophies. Constant praise and regular applause can be intoxicating. Some leaders become dependent upon it. It silences their insecurities. It medicates them by reducing the harshness of the stress of leadership and the pressure to accomplish.

When a perceived threat to our balance arrives, subconsciously we began to marginalize that threat. We look at it only as a perceived threat. In actuality, any genuine authentic team member who loves you and not your position or power is an ally, not a threat. Any pastor with a healthy self-image will recognize this. If you find an inexplicable inhibition to support team members under your supervision, particularly those young, charismatic, gifted people who God has assigned you to steward, your dysfunction is deeply seeded. At your core you must relinquish your grip and allow God to free you to be you, while you simultaneously mentor others to succeed under your tutelage.

Let's consider Saul in the Old Testament. Saul was a charismatic leader; a king the people respected for his gallant military victories and his success in freeing the land from its hereditary enemies, the Philistines. Saul's reign as king was saturated with constant warring against his foes, in all of which he proved victorious.

If you recall, the battle against the Amalekites was recorded with great detail. God had had enough of this particularly cruel and relentless foe of Israel. Saul was ordered to kill the entire population:

Now go, attack the Amalekites and totally destroy all that belongs to them. Do not spare them; put to death men and women, children and infants, cattle and sheep, camels and donkeys. (1 Samuel 15:3)

However, Saul made a terrible error in judgment. Consumed by his confidence in himself, he decided to destroy all of the Amalekites with the exception of the king and the best of the livestock. He assumed it would be a welcomed sacrifice to offer these spoils to the Lord as an offering. He was wrong. This displeased God. Samuel, a man of God, asked Saul, "How is it that you did not obey the Lord?"

Saul confessed that he killed all of the Amalekites except the king and the best of the livestock that they may be offered to the Lord as burnt offerings. Samuel responded, "Obedience is better than sacrifice." This was the test of Saul's ability to lead as king. Can you obey?

For rebellion is like the sin of divination, and arrogance like the evil of idolatry. Because you have rejected the word of the Lord, he has rejected you as king. (1 Samuel 15:23)

What a hard word. The spirit of the Lord departed from Saul. What a sad commentary on a great king who had the potential of being one of the greatest kings. The kingdom was torn from Saul and given to David. David was young, anointed, and a gifted hunter and shepherd. He was a type of "Hooper." Seasoned soldiers laughed at him. He was summarily dismissed as unqualified when the battle lines with the Philistines were drawn and the Israelite men were sent to war. Yet, David was anointed king.

I sense that just as in the times of old when God had enough of the oppressive Amalekites and their sin, He has had enough of the oppression of our youth. He's sending charismatic young leaders, like David, who will impact and lead the youth into success and significance. The challenge is: Which pastors will step up and humbly support these young leaders? Will the pastors obey the word of the Lord and help to utterly destroy the enemy or, by their own stubbornness, forfeit complete victory by holding on to their own way? If you, Pastor, reject the Lord in what you know to be true in these matters, God will reject you. Let it not be said of you that the "glory has departed," that God has removed His spirit because you could not be trusted to obey. Find the Davids (or Davettes) of your congregation who are gifted to war on behalf of the youth. Welcome them into leadership. Welcome their edgy ideas, out of the box methods, and creative strategies for reaching and growing a youth ministry. Get them the training they need. Secure for them the resources they need to execute the job. Join them in battle, and, whatever you do, don't work against them.

Hooper, after all, was just being Hooper. He was game for the hunt, passionate about sharks, knowledgeable, and relevant. Beseech the Father to reveal to you the Hooper that is present, or send to you and your flock the Hooper with a mission, who is looking to fulfill God's purposes.

Show me a Hooper who serves under a pastor committed to youth within a church community open to radically loving its youth and I'll show you a church destined to go to the next level in out of the box, uncommon youth ministry!

Questions for reflection:

1. Consider the skill sets of those who work with your youth ministry. Are you fully aware of the extent of their expertise?

2. What plans are in place at your church to ensure your youth workers are continually building into their own skill sets?

3. What opportunities do you give your youth ministry team to continually build their credibility among the youth they serve?

4. The answer to this question might sting. Pastor, are there areas where you have not exhibited full obedience to ensuring your youth workers have what is needed to reach those God has placed in *their* care?

Chapter 8
As Goes the Head, So Goes the Body

"I've been catching sharks for twenty years!" Quint declared.

When it comes to engaging, educating, and training youth in godliness, our past victories have little bearing on the qualifications needed to complete *today's* job. The youth culture is always changing. Popular and current youth slang quickly fades with time. Norms shift frequently and without warning. Pastor, don't get me wrong. The wealth of knowledge, experience, and God-given insight you've attained are indispensable. But I emphasize to you again: this is no ordinary shark! Any reliance on past experience can be leveraged by Satan to send you down the wrong road with the wrong approach at the wrong time. In his book *The Spiritual Man,*

Watchman Nee warns that relying upon past experience can be a trap set by Satan in order for us to miss fresh revelation.

Dr. Myles Munroe is so sensitive to his pursuit of fresh revelation that he says he changes his Bible every year so as not to allow his margin notes to prejudice his thoughts and understanding about a highlighted verse.

More than ever, the body of Christ, the church, His bride needs male and female leaders committed to relying on the Holy Spirit. We need pastoral leadership that is not solely based on the credentials of the academy or the applause of men. We need leadership hungry for the heart of God as it pertains to the redemption of our children with spiritual ears tuned to the still small voice of God.

After twenty years of catching sharks, Quint (again used as an example of a type of a pastor) has grown complacent. He showed no fire for the hunt. He became more concerned about providing a living for himself than eliminating a lethal threat to the people in his own community.

"Ten thousand dollars!" was his bid.

He was willing to earn the money, but was not concerned about saving the people. When the bottom line is an offering, a budget, or a financial seed, the shark will always win. I am a firm believer in tithing. My family and I have often been blessed because of our commitment to sow financially into the lives and ministries of others, and through our regular gifts and offerings to God's storehouse. I am motivated to tithe through obedience and my first expectation is to see lives impacted *because of* my gift, not so that my gift will get *me* more money. When did we digress to making money the bottom line? Remember the early days of your ministry? When you were on fire for God? When you preached with passion? When you only needed one suit? When you were willing to pay your own way? Remember when you were fulfilling your call with fervency? At one point in the early days you'd do ministry for free, wouldn't you? Does it profit a church to build a new edifice, finance extravagant outreach, and yet have little or no success in meeting the regular needs of the youth in its own house?

I'm not saying that other visions, passions for ministry, or pastoral convictions are subordinate to the demand for effective and comprehensive ministry to the youth. It's just that our youth are in CRISIS! We don't have the luxury to postpone securing the prerequisites needed for establishing a youth work. We need to make it a priority to establish the framework necessary to withstand the relentless spiritual warfare over the souls of our youth. We cannot subject the future of our youth to twenty-year-old paradigms.

We need a bigger boat!

The paradigm shift must begin with you, Pastor, and your leaders. The shift needs to be from egocentric to Christo-centric! Having the spirit of Christ at their center is what changed the disciples from ordinary fishermen to mighty men of great exploits. These are the last days. The time is coming when our direction will need to be so sensitive to the voice of Christ that if the command is to turn two degrees to the right, but we turn three degrees, we'll miss the blessing. We cannot depend upon experience, political correctness, or the voices of the people. It must be Christ and Christ alone. The crux of our success is, as Charles Finney says, "knowing what it means to be filled with the spirit of Christ, led by the spirit and to know what it means to be endued with power from on high."

What can we say of you, Pastor? What degree of the Holy Spirit do you enjoy? Have you forgotten to thirst and to hunger? He always fills and feeds those who come with an appetite for intimacy! Are you still knocking and asking or have your inquiries ceased years ago? Are you tired of the same sermons, lackluster worship and unenthused church members? We do not need the God of the impossible if our goals have been reduced solely to possible pursuits within our comfort zone. Of what use to us is a God that can accomplish the ridiculous simply with the wave of His hand, if leadership is leading by auto-pilot with no ingenuity, no cutting edge evangelism, and empty youth ministry? I am convinced that it pleases God to give us ambitious, out-of the-box ideas, greater than who we are, so that by stretching our faith he is afforded the joy of pulling the impossible within our reach. Are you even reaching?

Dare not approach this shark with carnal weapons. Quint was unmatched in his battle with the shark when he did it his way. Barrels! How utterly absurd to think he could stop, or even slow down, a two-ton, twenty-six-foot-long, man-eating shark by attaching a barrel, then two, and even three. Nonsense!

I have seen the investment some churches have put in their youth ministry. To use the word "investment" is absurd. Some students have a better sound system in the trunk of their car than what's used for the youth meeting. I've seen untrained and unprepared youth ministers scramble from week to week to "do something" with the youth. I recognize it because there was a time when that unprepared youth worker was me. Two of my favorite descriptions for our upcoming youth events were "special guest" and "surprise activity." It was a special guest because I didn't know who the guest was going to be. It was a surprise activity because I had yet to plan it. When I announced to the youth "next Friday was going to be a surprise," they didn't know it was going to be a surprise for me, too. I desperately needed training. Have you seen this need in your youth leadership? How spiritually sensitive have you been to the needs of your youth, or should I say the *cries* of your youth? What priority does your youth budget demand at the church council meetings?

There are pastors, thankfully, who are spot on. They are not concerned with their egos, with who gets the credit, whose name is first, above, biggest, or highlighted. They are only concerned about saving the lives of as many of their students and their students' friends as possible. They recognize the necessity to be intentional about hiring a fully vetted, passionate, and called youth worker. There are pastors who have done their homework. They have not only hired the right man or woman for the job, they have also provided resources for the youth leader to excel.

If that's you, Pastor, it is imperative for you to sound the alarm with your colleagues. In your pastoral circle of influence, raise the banner of commitment and investment into the lives of youth. Share your successes. The words of this author are of course that of a youth specialist, not a lead pastor. Please do not underestimate your influence. Pastors must hold one another accountable for the entire spectrum of the role of the under-shepherd. Caring for the body, shepherding the sheep is demanding with many challenges, pitfalls, and attacks. As we examine pastoral successes in serving our youth it's critical to keep in mind that some pastors often hear from many sources what they must do, however they will only listen to other pastors. I admit, there are many times I've heard the same bit of wisdom time and again from my wife but it never registered until a colleague expressed the same wisdom in a different setting. Then, it clicked! I then foolishly return to my wife and proclaim my discovery, to which she says in disbelief, "Isn't that the same thing I've been saying to you for weeks?"

Much of what has been said in this book I'm sure you have already heard. If possible, briefly suspend your knowledge of the author of this source. Humbly hear this plea instead as if it were coming from a caring colleague, a trusted voice. Maybe even the voice of that wise pastor you highly regard and respect. Now resolve that whatever the sacrifice, you will not return to business as usual in leading your congregation in loving your youth. There are those in your circles of leadership who need to witness your growth and success in this area, and they need to hear of said success from you.

This is not a matter of competition. "My youth group size is greater than yours!" That is exactly the kind of thinking that fosters wrong motives and becomes a hindrance to the voice of Christ. We must be willing to humble ourselves, learn all we can, and adapt all we can to succeed as best we can. Remember, this is no ordinary shark. While we argue, boast, and compare, this shark will eat our students alive. This shark has unprecedented access to our students.

Wireless technology has engulfed our youth in unmonitored access and communication with the world like never before. According to the website ProCon.org, forty-three percent of online sexual solicitors were identified as adolescents (under eighteen years old). Thirty percent were adults between the ages of eighteen and twenty-one, and nine percent were adults over the age of twenty-one (as of Dec. 31, 2008). That means seventy-three percent of online sexual solicitors are twenty-one or younger. The average teen will spend a minimum of nine hours a week on social networking sites, like Facebook. The time is even greater if you include time on a personal digital assistant (PDA), or smartphone. Today's teens may not be aware that the information they post on these sites is public and that photos and text can be retrieved even after deletion. Consequences from over-sharing personal information include vulnerability to sexual or financial predators and lost job opportunities when employers find these embarrassing photos or comments. Social networking sites have no way to verify that people are who they claim to be, leaving youth vulnerable to solicitations from online predators who are able to mask their true identities.

Here are some statistics that should leave you quaking in your boots. In February 2009, MySpace identified 90,000 registered sex offenders with profiles on its site, while Facebook declined to reveal how many were present on its site. Even if the sites agree to remove sex offenders, they cannot identify all of them or stop them from creating new accounts.

Today's teenager will witness 25,000 homicides on television before high school graduation. About one third of today's teens have been drunk in the last month.

Eight thousand teens will contract a sexually transmitted disease today. About one million teenagers are pregnant in America right now. Each year about 340,000 teens will get abortions. Approximately one of every ten teenage girls has been raped.

The average teen will see 14,000 sexual references on television this year. Nine out of ten teens have seen pornography online. Half of our teens are no longer virgins.

An estimated 1.6 million American children have become victims of the sex trade. The average age is between twelve and fourteen years old. Each year, 2.8 million teens run away from home. Within forty-eight hours of hitting the streets, one third will end up lured into prostitution or pornography.

One in five of our teens has attempted suicide. Over 1,500 kill themselves every year.

Fifty-three percent of teenagers today believe Jesus sinned. Eighty-three percent believe truth is relative. Sixty-five percent of teens today believe there is no way to tell which religions are true.

Today about half of the junior high and senior high students in America drink alcohol on a monthly basis. Alcohol is the most frequently used drug by youth in America. Marijuana is the most widely used illicit drug used by teens in America. Between 1991 and 2001, the percentage of eighth graders who used marijuana doubled from one in ten to one in five. Research indicates that the earlier teens start using marijuana, the more likely they are to become dependent on it, or other drugs, later in life.

All of this goes on while most of your students sit at home on youth meeting night, because your church youth program is whack. You need a bigger boat!

At a recent high school drug-free assembly the principal only invited the one hundred eighty students who he considered "at-risk." I lobbied for the full school assembly, but the principal declined, stating that only the at-risk students needed the presentation. The reality is, ALL OF OUR STUDENTS are at risk! It doesn't matter what community your church is in, the median income of your congregants, or the average number of degrees each family holds. Your students are at risk! A new curriculum will not save them, nor will a midnight basketball league. They don't need a new program, they need a new heart. Jesus IS the answer. The church IS His method. The people of God are the vehicle. Your leadership is the guide.

At my youth center in Washington, D.C., someone asked me how do I get so many students to participate in our program. The answer is simple, we open the door. We open the door and students encounter strategic, consistent, and compassionate youth ministry. We are relevant because we work at it. We are effective because we are trained. The students in your church and community are waiting. They are hungry for the revelation of purpose and mission. They are starving for healthy adult relationships, mentorship and discipleship. We must reap the harvest. The call to reach them is not only a challenge, it is also a warning. If you fail to reap the harvest, the crop will spoil. When I turn on the evening news or read the daily newspaper about another teenaged murderer, thief, or delinquent, I don't have the luxury of closing my eyes, shaking my head and murmuring "tsk, tsk, tsk." Those who fall through the cracks are not mere statistics, but rather crop that has spoiled. But by the grace of God, there go I.

Pastor, you must take the lead. Prioritizing

ministry to children and youth may seem risky at first. You may ask, "What are the returns?" Well, honestly, you may not see the returns during your tenure. You may wonder where the finances will come from. You may not know until you begin a journey that demands them. Either way, it's going to cost you. You can invest in prevention or pay for the struggle of rehabilitation after the fact. Do you ask, "What if we run out of money and have to slash the budget?" Without faith, it is IMPOSSIBLE to please God! You are only accountable for today, don't worry about tomorrow. Yes, plan and prepare for tomorrow, count the cost for tomorrow, but move by faith today. Whether you are doing great or not, there will always be someone not satisfied by your leadership; that's the fabric of life. How do I handle the naysayers? I remember that I am not called to be a crowd pleaser, but a God pleaser. So are you. You have been divinely appointed for this leadership position that you should lead for an audience of One. So as He which hath called you is holy, so be ye holy!

The aforementioned are all logical concerns. You may even feel vulnerable to the ridicule of colleagues who'd suggest this type of commitment to a youth program is untraditional and guaranteed to fail. I've faced all of these questions and the solution is simple. Yet, to these and other obstacles I charge you to lead on! You are the leader and, as God instructed Joshua, "Be strong and courageous!" (Joshua 1:9) How do we make this commitment in an area that seems fraught with uncertainty? With courage!

Dr. Myles Munroe declares, "An army of sheep led by a lion will defeat an army of lions led by a sheep every time!"

Bishop Milton Grannum of New Covenant Church of Philadelphia says that "success is our ability to fill our capacity."

The key ingredient is courage! When, as a young teen, Mary was told by the angel that the Holy Spirit would come upon her and she would conceive, she said, "Do it!" That's courage! Do it! Lead with courage. Dr. Grannum also writes, "If there is no precedent, set one!" Be courageous.

Pastor John Jenkins of the First Baptist Church of Glenarden in Prince George's County, Maryland is a shining example of this kind of courage. Recently Pastor Jenkins okayed a merger of the largest and most effective local youth ministry with his church's youth ministry. His words to the leader of that youth work, "Don't change what you are doing, because what you are doing is successful. Come and partner with us to make us better!"

Did you hear that? The pastor of a very large and growing church recognized a deficiency. Even though he had membership over thirteen thousand, a four thousand-seat auditorium, and a church that was voted the number one African American church in the country by the *Hoodie Awards*, he humbled himself and said, "Do it!" He reached out to another church who had sustained success in the area in which his church needed improvement. He said, "Help us get better!"

Remnant, the name of Zion Church's youth ministry, had been averaging four hundred to five hundred teens in attendance each Friday night for an unforgettable evening of relevant urban youth ministry and outreach. They had developed a remarkably effective strategy to impact urban students for Christ. They worked out the details and partnered with Pastor Jenkins for a win-win for the youth of the community. Pastor Jenkins hosted a meeting for adults at his church interested in volunteering their time and support for such a bold undertaking. Over one thousand and three hundred people showed up! Courage! At the time of this observation, that merger (called Merge) is averaging three thousand students every other week for their main event! Mediocrity has lulled the masses into complacency. We accept an ineffective, tradition-bound, lifeless youth program because we've prematurely conceded defeat. God is not dead, He's alive!

Oswald Chambers writes, "The weakest saint can experience the power of the Deity of the Son of God once he is willing to 'let go.' Any strand of our own energy will blur the life of Jesus. We have to keep letting go, and slowly and surely the great full life of God will invade us in every part, and men will take knowledge of us that we have been with Jesus."

Do you realize that all of the resources of heaven are at your disposal, but there has yet to arise a vision that places a demand on God to fulfill the financial need? God has cattle on a thousand hills and a million possible ways to finance your youth program. All you need is one.

Part of the thrill of the hunt in the movie *JAWS* was anticipating the manner in which the shark would ultimately be destroyed, if at all. The audience had no idea how this thrill-ride would end. Bullets didn't work, barrels didn't work, and drowning the shark didn't work. But in the end, the shark was killed! There was a way. I don't know the particulars of your church leadership situation or how you will defend the youth of your church and community against this shark. I do know that God has a plan and a purpose for you to initiate comprehensive and effective ministry to the youth that's capable of sustained growth and health. The mantle of leadership is on you. Exchange your burden with God, for His burden is light. God is a God of faith and action. We are to believe and act while God honors our faith by moving favorably on our behalf. Are you prepared to see God show up in a supernatural way? Are you motivated to place a demand on God for insight, human resources, and uncommon provision? If so, then declare, "No more status quo!" Stand on the promises already spoken to you, mighty leader of great valor! Ask, seek, knock, and it shall be given. You shall find and the door will be opened for you.

Questions for reflection:

1. How many youth drop off your church's radar each year? How many return?

2. What are the statistics for teen pregnancy, school drop-out rates, teen misdemeanor and felony charges, youth-related alcohol and drug use in your area?

3. What other ministries are seeking to reach the same youth as you are in your community?

4. Are there realistic ways in which you can partner with someone who is already experiencing success in an area in which your church needs help?

Pastor, We Need A Bigger Boat!

Chapter 9 | Who's on Watch?

After the first shark attack, Chief Brody erected tall, extremely obvious, watchtowers. They stood at least ten to fifteen feet higher than the highest lifeguard stand. From this advantaged point and equipped with a watch guard, bell, walkie-talkie, and binoculars, the chief and his team were set to signal the Amity beach-goers of any waterborne danger at a moment's notice. As quickly as the towers were manned and the beaches were opened, Chief Brody was under fire from his boss, the mayor.

"Have you lost your mind, Chief?" he screamed. "Reporters are here! It's all psychological. You yell 'barracuda' everyone's says, 'Huh? What?' You yell 'shark' and we've got a panic on our hands on the fourth of July!"

Chief Brody was not interested in the opinions of the masses. The chief was not concerned about the celebration of another traditional holiday. He was concerned about the citizens of Amity.

There comes a time when the applause, the shouting, the dancing, and whooping must be silenced so that the matters of life and death in our churches can be addressed. A true believer in his assignment, Chief Brody had on his mind the safety and well-being of the citizens of Amity, their children, and the thousands of vacationers. There's a sense of uneasy defenselessness when one is swimming in the great expanse of open water at the beach. With a known predator in the water, the chief, unwilling to venture into the water himself, felt an intense obligation to watch. He had to watch for the child who may have wandered from the inattentive eye of a parent or guardian. He watched for any abnormal disturbance of the shoreline. He watched for the unmistakable prominent dorsal fin of the great white shark. The mayor, conversely, was awash with the fear of summer failure, and the prospect of shark mania driving the tourists and their resources away.

The mayor looked at the same beaches that the chief did, but unfortunately he was unable to see the vulnerability. The shark attacks were not frequent, but isn't one death too many? If all professional predictions were correct, this shark was going to make an example out of this small town. The shark was just going to do what sharks of this type and species do. Feed. Lurking, waiting, and patiently swimming for its next victim, the shark was definitely in the water. There was no way of predicting where this bottomless stomach would rear its grizzly head filled with deadly teeth. Only one thing was sure, its appetite would anchor this eating-machine in Amity until the food supply was gone. The chief knew this as a result of his cursory study of the long-bodied marine fish. Trying to convince the mayor of the gravity of the situation was futile.

Who's on watch for our children? They are the most vulnerable in a world of predators, and in a culture replete with wrong messages, the wrong means, and the wrong methods. Someone must be on watch for them. In Amity, it was Chief Brody's job. Of course his job came with a job description. He was probably one of several candidates. There was a vetting process that included a background check, consideration of his prior work experience, and obtaining references. The chief applied for this job because he wanted it. His charge was to serve and protect the citizens of Amity. When it comes to caring for children, one would assume the same commitment and passion were true for parents. Sadly, it is not always the case.

Parents are not given a job description, and not all know how to watch for their young. No prior experience is necessary. Even those with experience may have failed the first time and repeat the same mistakes with each subsequent child. There is no credit check, background check, or phone calls made to a list of trusted references. Many children are the product of unwanted pregnancies, they suffer at the hands of inadequate parenting, and are surrounded by adult failure. In the wake of these adverse circumstances, they must also deal with the world and its unforgiving swiftness. Who's watching for them? Who is keeping a watchful eye for the wandering youth who has strayed from an inattentive parent? Who's watching for the unusual disturbance in the water? Who's watching for the unmistakable prominent dorsal fin of the great white shark? What trained eye is scanning the young to prevent the attempted suicide?

The traps, disillusionments, misconceptions, and disenfranchisement of youth are there. The lure of mood-altering drugs is there, hiding behind a so-called friend who is in actuality a "frenemy" (a friend to the face but an enemy to the future). Who's watching?

Recognize this: Your youth minister has applied for the job of watchman. The youth minister has surrendered to the background checks and has supplied a list of references so that he might follow the call to stand in the gap for the young. The youth minister is prepared to watch, because God has given him or her eyes to see! In far too many churches, it's the hidden agendas of the "powers that be" that complicate efforts to guard our youth. The youth worker cannot equip youth effectively with power to stand, believe, and cope, because some in his or her church are in disagreement with the necessary expense to do so.

At least the chief could erect towers, hire staff, and equip his staff with all that the peculiarities the assignment required. For the youth minister, there is no budget, there is no youth program priority, he or she is standing watch for the relentless predator because mom is asleep on the couch, church leadership looks but cannot see, and the youth are aimlessly searching for their destiny. If such a state of blindness persists, your church vitality will be suffocated. It will die from lack of fresh oxygen. That oxygen is the by-product of the next generation. The church of tomorrow, which we would all claim to be working toward, will evaporate from our communities.

Questions for reflection:

1. In your community, what ministries or organizations have tried, but failed, to be successful reaching youth?

2. Are there identifiable reasons you could observe as contributing to their failure?

3. How would you rate your church's success level in the following areas?

Understanding the issues facing your youth.

Flexibility in adjusting methods when a program or technique is identified as ineffective.

Honesty among decision-makers when it comes to talking about youth's problems.

Commitment to being a part of the youth workers' support team. (Instead of simply being someone they report to.)

Provision of mentoring to those working with youth.

Chapter 10 | The End-ing

Our favorite feature film comes to a close when the words "The End" appear on the movie screen. Those of us who have seen the movie *JAWS* know that the end is remarkable and exciting. I am going to assume at this point you've seen the movie. If not, be forewarned, this chapter comes with a spoiler alert. I will disclose how the movie ends. The details of *JAWS* epic ending provide an illuminating revelation for our analogy.

My impetus for writing this book has not been merely to bring appreciation for a classic movie or to sow acrimony into the pastor-youth minister relationship. Let me be clear, this work has been a divine appointment. For ten years I've presented this information as a workshop. It was effective in its own right, but not entirely developed in thought and scope. Initially my thoughts were limited to the characters and the unforgettable phrase, "We need a bigger boat." But as I pen this final chapter, I am extraordinarily aware of how the Holy Spirit has brought to light a pointed, comprehensive message to you, Pastor. How have you encountered these words? How did this book come into your possession? Was it coincidence or a God-incidence? You must take inventory of the words that have pricked your heart. Where, within these pages, did you recognize yourself and sense an unmistakable stirring? Do you just walk away? Or do you respond as David, who was hungry for a greater reality:

Search me, God, and know my heart; test me and know my anxious thoughts. See if there is any offensive way in me, and lead me in the way everlasting. (Psalm 139:23-24)

Oswald Chambers says that if ever it's important enough for God to dispatch His precious Holy Spirit to quicken our hearts, then it ought to be important enough for us to hear and take heed to that which has been revealed.

Let's get back to the movie. In desperation, Hooper entered the water, secured in a lightweight cage. The plan was to get close enough to the shark to fire a dart gun loaded with an anesthetic into the soft tissue of the killer shark's mouth. It was an extremely risky ambition filled with uncontrollable variables. The very place that had been synonymous with death, the water, was the very place Hooper was going to enter. The crew had no choice. There was no other option. *The Orca* was disabled. The engine was beyond repair. Water was filling the hull of the ship hastily, eliminating valuable minutes before the entire crew would be in the water. By the time the fulcrum was in place and the cage was in the water, from out of the dark of the sea the shark appeared. His first violent crash into the cage dislodged the dart gun from Hooper's grasp. In a badly dented and broken cage, a panicked Hooper faced the shark as it returned for another attempt to devour him. The cage was so damaged it permitted the snout of the shark complete access to its defenseless victim. A resourceful Hooper grabbed the hunting knife attached to his belt.

As the shark tried desperately to get his viselike jaws locked on its prey, Hooper unleashed a frenzied knife attack on the predator. This effort was enough of a distraction to the shark, prompting it to momentarily retreat before coming back for what was going to undoubtedly be the kill. Simultaneously, the crew, in response to the violent commotion under water, began to reel in the cage. In the tumult of the cage's movement and the shark's retreat, Hooper was able to slip out of the cage and hide in the reef on the ocean floor, eluding the great white shark's detection.

The shark then turned its focus to the sinking *Orca*. With one huge heave, it lunged out of the ocean onto the stern of the boat. Everything unsecured on the deck was destined for the jaws of this man-eating monster, including the crew.

The Orca was now pointing more vertically than horizontally under the unforgiving weight of the great white shark beached on its stern. Chief Brody held on for dear life as he watched in terror while Quint succumbed to the inevitable. With every desperate ounce of effort, Quint hopelessly struggled to grasp any part of *The Orca* within reach, but to no avail. He slipped and slid downward toward the open mouth of the shark on a water-soaked, slick deck. Quint slowly glided right into the mouth of the shark, legs first. The shark, unfazed by Quint's erratic kicking, violently chomped Quint at the waist before swallowing him whole.

The chief, helpless, watched in horror as this relentless eating machine swallowed Quint in two bites. *The Orca* was nearly completely submerged. Only the mast was visible, total submersion was imminent, and the shark was still hungry.

Like Quint, the church that is most hardened against the necessity of change for the sake of its youth will most likely be the first to be swallowed up by irrelevancy. Full of dread, Chief Brody prepared for his turn at the inevitable, a return to the water. When the shark returned to the sinking *Orca*, Chief Brody was able to lodge one of Hooper's compressed air oxygen tanks into its jaws. The shark retreated again briefly then made another determined attempt for the chief.

Armed only with a rifle and a few bullets, the chief knows he needs to get as close as possible to the water to lure the shark. He needed to get much too close for comfort to increase his probability of shooting the tank in its mouth. After two misses, the chief, with his last shot and at the last second, shoots the tank, which was now deep within the mouth of the fast-approaching shark. The detonation sends two tons of bloody shark meat exploding into the air. Hooper returns to the surface and reconnects with the chief.

In the final scene, Hooper and the chief use Quint's barrels as a makeshift float to return to the distant beaches of Amity, while seabirds feasted on the kill. The nightmare was over.

Do not miss this point: The captain of *The Orca*, the veteran fisherman, the self-righteous shark hunter, the one with all of the answers and ego, the guy unwilling to listen to others, was the only one on the boat who was swallowed by the shark! What if we do not change? What if we, like Quint, ignore the warnings and run the red lights? By God's grace we are afforded examples, admonitions, and even a door of escape from our temptations so that our progress will continue and our success will remain. But what if we disregard the signs? If we fail to make the progressive turn in our churches, will we be among the first swallowed up by irrelevancy?

I think it's important to define irrelevant here. In two words, irrelevant simply means "not applicable." Synonyms for irrelevancy prove also to be revealing:

immaterial, neither here nor there, unrelated, inappropriate, beside the point, and extraneous. Extraneous is defined as coming from outside.

Quint came from outside. His world was outdated, not applicable, antiquated, and obsolete. His strategy was inappropriate, his boat was archaic, and his thinking was out-of-date. In the moments of his death, his effort was still to cling to his unsuitable boat. When the new way encounters the old way, something's got to give or catastrophe will result.

Jesus said it a little differently when He reminded us that you cannot put new wine into old wineskins. Once the new wine is put into old, rigid, inflexible, unyielding wineskins and begins to ferment and expand, the old wineskins crack and burst. The new wine and all of its benefit pours to the ground. Its value is lost. It is of no use.

New wine must be put into new wineskins. New wineskins are flexible enough to accommodate the expansion of the new wine as it ferments. The new wine then shapes the new wineskin. The new wine becomes available for use and maintains its value.

Church leadership possessing the unyielding commitment to tradition and hardened disposition will inevitably produce tragic results. The church's new wine, unable to be integrated into the life of the church, will depart in search for receptive new attitudes progressive enough to dream and grow within; "new wineskins" if you will.

After the new wine has departed, the few that stay

behind, like the seabirds of *JAWS*, are reduced to eating the remains of the carcass left by leadership with no vision.

We cannot allow our ministry to be trapped in the familiar. Churches that exist only within that which is safe forfeit fulfilling the great commission. Bishop Don Meares put it this way, "When a pastor fails to radically reach out to the generation on his heels, the median age of the congregation will eventually grow to become the same as that of the pastor and the church will lose the next generation."

"As Christians we must be willing to be led beyond our familiar groups so we can touch those who are in other settings," noted pastor and preacher Dr. James Massey exhorts.

Known by many as the greatest evangelist of our time, Billy Graham elucidates further, "The message of the Gospel never changes. For good reason, God never changes. And neither does our basic spiritual need nor His answer to that need. The methods of preaching that message do change and in fact, they must change. If we fail to bridge the gap between us and those we must reach, our message will not be communicated and our efforts will be in vain." We must bridge the gap, for if we do not, we fail God!

Simon had been fishing all night and was washing his nets when the master got into his boat, pushed off from shore, and began teaching. When He finished, He invited Simon to head to the deep and cast down his nets once again. I can only imagine what must have flashed through Simon's mind, some of which he allowed to slip out of his mouth.

"We've been fishing ALL NIGHT and have caught NOTHING (emphasis mine), but since you've ASKED, we'll let down our nets again."

What we didn't hear may have sounded a little more like this: "How is this carpenter in MY boat going to tell ME, Simon, to cast down my nets again? The fish are never hungry at this time of day! Doesn't he know how long I've been fishing? This is my life, I've been doing it for years. Before that, my daddy fished, as did his daddy before that! The Fish Shack down the road awarded me *Fisherman of the Year* more than any other fisherman in Galilee! Now this guy gets in my boat, in front of all of my people, asking me to let down my nets in the deep? I just cleaned my best nets and since I know this is not going to work, I'm going to grab my good nets, not my best, and get this little experiment over and done."

According to Luke chapter 5, there were so many fish, the nets began to break! They called to their friends to help. The two boats were so full of fish they began to sink. They quickly pulled their boat out of the water and onto the shore. Simon fell on his knees before Jesus. He was repentant. He, his brother, and companions were astonished at what happened. They left everything to follow Jesus that day.

Have you been toiling long hours, getting up early, and staying up late, but getting nothing? Has your catch been incommensurate to your effort? Or are you busting at the seams because the "fish" are overflowing? Before Jesus even got into the boat, He knew Simon Peter had been out all night. Jesus was aware of a reality that He needed Simon to experience. Jesus knew that reality would never materialize while Simon remained safely on the shore. He needed Simon to launch out into the deep. He needed Simon to cast his nets when and where they needed to be cast!

Maybe God has been waiting on you to hear HIS direction. Not to follow the safe, shore-bound way, but to take the risky, faith-filled, launch-out-into-the-deep way. When was the last time you "left the shore" with a decision or direction? How many years have you been stuck doing the *good* thing, while missing the *best* thing in God? Lean not, lean not, lean not on your own understanding, but in all thy ways acknowledge HIM! Resist, resist, resist the devil and he will flee!

Proverbs 3:5 and James 4:7 are two of the most conveniently misquoted verses in the Bible! We quote part "b" of each at the expense of the prerequisite words in part "a."

Proverbs 3:5a states: "Trust in the Lord with all your heart."

James 4:7a states: "Submit yourselves, then, to God."

How do we launch out into the deep? We trust Him, we humble ourselves, and we submit. This mandate is first to the leader, then to the flock! To lead we must go to the deep, and trust Him there. He knows where the increase, the fruit, and the fish are. Just as

Chief Brody ultimately had to go back to the water to find his victory, Jesus calls us to the deep to find ours. With that mammoth shark chomping away to reach the chief, the chief resourcefully threw the tank of compressed air into its mouth.

Get in position to make a difference, and use what you've got! Use who you've got! The time is getting short. Our enemy is bolder and hearts of the young are colder. Churches have tragically become more indifferent than ever regarding effective ministry to youth. Position your church to go against the flow of those who are content to simply placate general expectations of youth ministry. I have heard youth ministers voice their pastor's defense of the lack of investment into the youth program. When do we get beyond our excuses? My late pastor, Dr. Sam Hines, rebuked me one day early in my work as his youth pastor. When questioned about a failed assignment, I offered my excuse. His response: "Stephen, excuses are merely explanations of our ignorance." Today, we are too informed to claim ignorance. Instead we must mark the course, set the goal, and act!

God is so passionate about our fulfillment that He has a plan for non-action. He knows our destiny is the deep. He also knows of our reluctance and shore-bound contentment. He sees us in our boat, tied to the pier, falling short of his best. By His grace, He will allow a hurricane to enter the harbor. The winds will dislodge our tiny boat, and we eventually end up in the deep anyway. Mother eagles do this too. When the mother eagle builds her nest she always begins with thorns, broken branches, and rocks. She then covers these objects with leaves, fur from animals she's killed, and anything else soft and suitable that she finds. This comfortable environment is the perfect place for the babies to be born. When she sends them out to establish their independence initially they always come back. But then she knows it is time for them to leave the comfort of the nest for greater things. She's forced to dig into the nest with her talons to remove the soft carpet she's constructed. The next time the baby eagles return, the nest is a different place! Ouch! That was a thorn. Ouch! That was a broken branch. Ouch! That was a rock. It may be difficult for momma eagle to see her babies bleeding, but she knows a greater good will come of it. The baby eagles, grown enough to be on their own, leave for good to fulfill their destiny! That's often how God deals with our reluctance to lead.

Beware of the path of least resistance. It may be because you and the devil are headed in the same direction. That which is comfortable can lead to reluctance to go for God's best. At times God must allow thorns to provoke us so we sit up and take notice of Him. Have you had some "Ouches?" Ouch! That was another family leaving the church because the church had become irrelevant. Ouch! That was the resignation of another staffer because the pay had become too intermittent. Ouch! You fill in the blank.

There will always be pain. There is the pain of discipline and the pain of regret. The pain of regret leads to discouragement. The pain of discipline leads to a greater and a more fulfilling reality. Choose and then be strong.

Amity ended in a better place than it was in when that great white shark first showed up. The people of Amity learned to maximize their beach access. They gained new confidence in their Chief. Tourists returned. Shops once again bustled with summer activity. The Chief developed a better understanding of sharks because of his experience. Because of his new friendship with Hooper, he became better equipped to handle the water-born threats to his community.

What about the people in your Amity? What is their impression of you and your commitment to your youth? Today is the day and now is the time to declare and establish your stance on ministry to your youth. Begin your investment in a bigger boat today. Change your paradigm. It's not merely your youth service workers calling for a bigger boat. It's not just the silent cries of the needy youth calling for a bigger boat. It's not just the paranoid parent, feeling helpless in the struggle to raise her teen, calling for a bigger boat. If you listen carefully you can hear the still small voice of He who first called you saying, "Pastor, we need a bigger boat!"

A question:

You'll notice that at the end of each of the previous chapters, I've included questions for reflection to get your mind turning. My prayer is that you have begun to analyze the current state of affairs within your youth ministry and your community. I also pray that the Holy Spirit has ignited a fire and a renewed passion for the youth in your community. I pray this fire and passion becomes the genesis for revival that shows up in the freshness of new life for your church and community.

This last question is not meant to be merely reflected upon, but is a two-part question for action:

What does a bigger boat look like for your church, and what are you going to do in order to build it?

About the Author

Steve Fitzhugh is a nationally recognized speaker, author, and long-time champion for youth. He has served as youth pastor, assembly speaker, camp and convention keynote speaker and offers expertise in "all things youth."

Steve has been the president of PowerMoves since its inception in 1997. PowerMoves is the umbrella by which Steve commands his communications skill set to inspire, motivate, and educate youth. Steve is also the co-founder of The House, an after school teen drop-in center in the Anacostia community of Southeast Washington, D.C. There, he, along with his colleagues, transformed three former crack houses into a state-of-the-art youth teen center in one of the city's most underserved neighborhoods. He is also the national spokesperson for the Fellowship of Christian Athlete's One Way 2 Play Drug-free program, and is a part of Tony Dungy's All-Pro Dads program.

Steve can be found each year on over 150 middle school, high school, and college campuses articulating the tenets of the drug-free lifestyle. With over thirty years experience in working with teens, Steve's insights are clear, his knowledge base broad, and his effectiveness proven. His personal mantra, "Create a moment for life change, and God can change any life in a moment," provides the inspiration for his relentless and passionate advocacy for the youth of America.

Reach Steve through his website: www.PowerMoves.org

Also by Steve Fitzhugh:

Bringing the H.E.A.T. A Pocket Guide for Healthy, Effective, Attractive, Transforming Youth Ministry is a resource to light the fire for youth workers, youth ministers, and volunteers.

It provides practical strategies based on Steve's 30+ years of experience working with teens. Pastors, this is a guide your youth ministry team will turn to time and again as they seek to build an eternal, kingdom mindset in the youth of your church.

Touch Publishing
ISBN: 978-0-9937951-0-7

The Adventures of Lil' Stevie is a collection of stories taken from Steve's actual childhood adventures. This book series, for kids ages 7 - 14, provides loads of humor and excitement while kids learn valuable lessons from a young Steve Fitzhugh.

With memorable characters and situations kids can relate to, Steve teaches kids that they can be the star of their very own adventure: life! And along the way, the choices we make impact the kind of life we live.

Touch Publishing
ISBN: 978-0-9919839-1-9

Who Will Survive? Teenagers Struggle to Win the Ultimate Battle is an intriguing, insightful, and disturbing look at the plight of the 21st century teenager.

Today's teens are ruled by peer acceptance and lost in the haze of conformity, which grows darker each day. Where are the solutions? Who has the answers? When will our nation's young halt self-destruction?

Through this book, parents and students will be provoked to make the determination to be survivors.

Touch Publishing
ISBN: 978-0-9937951-1-4

www.ingramcontent.com/pod-product-compliance
Lightning Source LLC
LaVergne TN
LVHW041627070426
835507LV00008B/495